A Life Through the Lens

A Life Through the Lens

Memoirs of a Film Cameraman

ALAN HUME

with Gareth Owen

FOREWORDS BY
PETER ROGERS AND KEVIN CONNOR

McFarland & Company, Inc., Publishers
Jefferson, North Carolina, and London

All images used in this book are from Alan Hume's personal collection, unless otherwise stated.

Thanks to John Herron and Canal + Image (UK) Ltd. for permission to reproduce images from their archive.

The James Bond films are made by Eon Productions Ltd., and the views and opinions expressed herein are not necessarily shared by the producers.

LIBRARY OF CONGRESS CATALOGUING-IN-PUBLICATION DATA

Hume, Alan. 1924–
A life through the lens : memoirs of a film cameraman / Alan Hume with Gareth Owen ; forewords by Peter Rogers and Kevin Connor.
p. cm.
Includes index.

ISBN 0-7864-1803-6 (softcover : 50# alkaline paper) 

1. Hume, Alan, 1924– 2. Cinematographers—Great Britain—Biography. I. Owen, Gareth. II. Title.
TR849.H86H86 2004
778.5'3'092—dc22 2004007083

British Library cataloguing data are available

Manufactured in the United States of America

On the cover: Movie camera lens ©2004 PhotoDisc; Alan Hume.

McFarland & Company, Inc., Publishers
Box 611, Jefferson, North Carolina 28640
www.mcfarlandpub.com

For my darling Sheila—the light of my life

Acknowledgments

Special thanks to the following:

My chum Gareth Owen, for making sense of my ramblings and for his belief that there would be something interesting amongst them.

Peter Rogers, for offering me my break as a lighting cameraman in the first place, and for writing such a smashing foreword in the second.

Kevin Connor for many happy years' collaboration, and indeed his kindness in penning another foreword.

Barbara Broccoli and Michael G. Wilson at Eon Production for their kindness in allowing us to reproduce James Bond photographs.

Andy Boyle for his technical assistance in the scanning and saving all the photographs, and sorting out computer glitches.

And of course to all my friends and colleagues in the business—I couldn't have managed anything without the terrific support and help of so many wonderful crews!

—A.H.

Contents

Foreword

by Peter Rogers

I have known Alan Hume almost as long as I have known myself. I've known him as a giggling camera operator and as one of the film industry's foremost lighting cameramen.

I say giggling operator because when we were working on the early *Carry On* films, he giggled so much at the scenes he was shooting that he had to leave the stage to recover.

I've also known him as a non-giggling operator as, for instance, when he was shooting a scene lying flat on his stomach hanging out of a doorless helicopter and holding a hand-held camera.

Nothing was ever impossible for Alan. I remember an occasion during the filming of *Carry On Jack*. The scene depicted Kenneth Williams, who had fallen over and hurt himself and was surrounded by officers administering to his broken leg or whatever it was. I fancied a little indulgence, which was usual, and asked Alan to copy the famous painting of the Death of Nelson. I don't suppose anybody notices the parallel when they see the film, but Alan did it perfectly.

He became a lighting cameraman by accident or, as you might say, through someone else's fortune that became a misfortune. The regular cameraman on the *Carry On* films had the offer to light a film that included a 14-week location in Turkey. The *Carry On* was due to start shooting on the Monday and the man rang me on the Sunday to say he'd had this wonderful offer and would I release him. In the circumstances, I couldn't stand in his way, considering that my whole film would occupy only six weeks. So I was faced, on that Sunday, with the problem of finding a cameraman for the following day. I had what I thought was a brainwave. That is, a rush of think-of-it to the cranium. I phoned Alan

Tea time: taking a few minutes out of their busy schedule on set, Peter Rogers (left) and Gerald Thomas indulge in the legendary British tea break.

at his home and asked him if he was prepared to light the *Carry On* on the Monday instead of merely operating. He grabbed the opportunity with both hands and feet, and from that date he has never looked back, having photographed everything from *Carry On* to Bond and *Star Wars*. He has earned for himself the reputation of a first-class lighting cameraman, respected by his peers. (The film and the location in Turkey fell through and was never made. One man's meat is another man's poison.)

I used to call Alan the perennial juvenile because he never seemed to age. He always looked as though he didn't need to shave. His sons are in the film industry. They are both on the camera in one capacity or another, and on one particular *Carry On* I had the whole family with me—Alan lighting and his sons on camera. It was a very proud moment for me.

Foreword

by Kevin Connor

I had the very great fortune to have Alan Hume recommended to light my first feature film, *From Beyond the Grave.* Such was his kindness and patience with the rookie director, that I had further good luck in having his collaboration on my next six films.

To work alongside such a talented artist was an untold benefit that educated me through my early days. This friendship extended into his sons, Martin and Simon, also first-class camera technicians in their own right.

Looking back on those halcyon days, I remember only too well his tales from past movie adventures, his laughter echoing around the set with the crew invariably on their knees clutching stomachs, gasping for air.

Every day was a delight to work alongside this wonderful human being.

Introduction

Alan Hume BSC is a name synonymous with both British and World Cinema. He has served as director of photography on over 100 films and TV shows, and in lesser capacities on a further 50.

He has "lit" some of the greatest stars to ever stand in front of a motion picture camera: Bette Davis, Jon Voight, Noël Coward, Richard Attenborough, James Mason, Alec Guinness, Ann Todd, Trevor Howard, Louis Hayward, Deborah Kerr, Van Johnson, Peter Cushing, Christopher Lee, John Mills, Peter Finch, Roger Moore, Doug McClure, Harrison Ford, Joe Don Baker, Robert Mitchum, Faye Dunaway, Michael Caine, Anthony Hopkins, Hugh Grant, and Joan Collins. He is responsible for the "look" of some of the most successful films ever made, not least three James Bond adventures, *Return of the Jedi* and *A Fish Called Wanda.*

He has a unique insight into moviemaking, having worked with directors such as David Lean, Richard Marquand, John Glen, Jack Gold, Gerry Thomas, Andrei Konchalovsky, Edward Dmytryk, Ken Annakin, Lewis Gilbert, Freddie Francis...

With his wicked sense of humor and easygoing personality, he is able to relate stories of making movies, working with directors and stars, and the locations he was often dispatched to at short notice and sometimes for many months, with great good humor and insight, and without ever being over-technical or stuffy.

With over 50 years in the business, Alan Hume now opens his memories and photo albums and shares his life through the lens.

—G.O.

I

In at the Deep End

It was June 1976 and I was standing on the top of a totally perpendicular piece of rock on Baffin Island, north of Canada. It was 3,000 feet high, covered in snow and with a sheer drop. The weather had been pretty lousy and cloud rarely lifted off the rock. It seemed a million miles away from the main unit at Pinewood Studios in London, and the warmth of my family home just a few miles away from there.

I was there with a second unit camera team for the James Bond film *The Spy Who Loved Me* and its exciting pre-title sequence. John Glen was directing and I was the director of photography on the unit—the guy responsible for how the whole thing looked on film. A short time earlier, we'd flown out to this far peninsula and thought it the perfect location for the nail-biting ski stunt that was to open the film, but standing on that mountain going snowblind—as everything around us was totally white—I wondered if we'd made the right decision.

Timing was everything, not least with the light available. We knew that it would take about two hours to set up and film the jump from the time we got "thumbs up." As the light was gone off the mountain by 2 P.M., our days were short.

Ten days passed and we hadn't achieved the conditions we needed to film. My camera crew were poised liked coiled springs—we had three cameras out there with us, including one in a helicopter—and so with time ticking on, we decided to base ourselves at the foot of the mountain so as to reduce preparation time. Tents were flown in for us from Montreal and we set up camp. It was so cold that we moved into just one of the three tents, huddling together in order to keep warm. It was a small, tight-knit crew including Rick Sylvester (the stunt skier), a doctor, my camera operator Brian Elvy, a Canadian camera operator and two mountaineers.

The weather worsened and two weeks passed by without us capturing a single foot of film. I wouldn't say we were pressured by the production office back in London, as being so remote they weren't able to reach us by telephone, but I think we were all painfully aware that our being there was costing the production significantly. It was decided that rather than freeze to death, we'd take the helicopter back to our base in Pangnirtung each night.

Another week passed and John Glen decided that it might be useful to film some sequences of Rick skiing on neighboring mountains. It could be useful for cut-away shots later and, more importantly, it boosted our morale. It was during one of these few days on a neighboring rock that our helicopter pilot Bill Henderson suggested the cloud was lifting and the time was right. After so many weeks of preparing and anticipating this jump, I suddenly felt the blood rush from my face. This was it, and it was a far cry from my working diet of comedy and modest budget dramas back in London.

All was ready on the mountain. Safety checks were made. Cameras were set up. I jumped on board my camera helicopter, our Canadian camera operator mounted his camera under the huge precipice, and John was with Brian on the third camera. The light was fading fast. It really was now or never. With that, John signaled Rick Sylvester and told him "remember you are James Bond."

This was my first experience of James Bond and, for that matter, big-budget films. We all sat nervously awaiting the feedback from our rushes. It could either signal the start of many more great things, or end our careers there and then.

Mercifully, the response was jubilant and the ski-jump in the opening sequence of *The Spy Who Loved Me* was one of the few times I've ever seen a cinema audience go deadly silent, before standing up to give an ovation.

Things were looking up.

But how did I get started in this mad business, you ask? It's an interesting little story which I'll now share with you, and James Bond will feature again quite significantly later on.

II

Action!

In the dark days of 1939 when World War II broke out, youngsters in London and its surrounds were evacuated to safer areas, away from the main thrust of the expected Luftwaffe bombings. I was evacuated to Reading in Berkshire, which wasn't too far from home and was quite countrified in places—ideal for a growing lad. It was there I finished my schooling, or not actually. I went to a local school with a class of 100-plus others. Overcrowding was an accepted situation, not just in Reading but all over the country as most of Britain's main (and industrial) cities were evacuated. There were tens of thousands of children on the move. Whilst the whole experience was a great education, I learned very little academically; and so it would be fair to say that my formal education ended when I was 15.

The first year of the War was quiet. In fact, it was dubbed "The Phoney War." The anticipated danger, and I guess for a 15-year-old *excitement* of danger, was nowhere to be seen. It was agreed that I should return home to my family and friends, and so my bags were packed and I headed for the railway station.

Very soon after my return to the family bosom, and after my stipulation that I was done with school, I had to think about work. But what as? I had no real aspirations, but my father was keen I follow him onto the railway, and in particular, London Underground. I couldn't think of any other options, and it seemed like a decent enough company to work for with prospects.

I was signed up as a stores-boy at London Underground's Acton works. I'd catch the train in from Uxbridge, in West London, every day and then back home every night. It became a routine and to be honest, a bit of a grind. I can't say it was a job I liked, but I stayed with it …

what else was there? Well, there *was* something, actually. One of the chaps I occasionally spoke with on the train to Acton mentioned that he worked at a film laboratory around the corner, Olympic Film Labs, and that they were looking for young men—as most of the men had been called up for the forces—and would I be interested?

The idea instantly appealed. I don't know why, but it was like a light bulb being switched on in my head. I'd always been interested in photography—nothing elaborate you understand, just Box Brownie stuff. I arranged an interview, and before I knew it I'd landed a job as a general go-fer, running around with the cans of film and doing other jobs as and when. It was actually a very valuable grounding, because I crossed the floor at all levels in all departments and got to know quite a lot about the place and the people there. Every evening the van driver who collected the film from the studios would bring it back to the lab. He would go to Denham and Pinewood Studios and back through Uxbridge—so I asked if I could go with him one Friday, and get dropped off at home at the end. I was desperately curious about film studios, what they looked like and how they all worked. I'd been a big film fan and regular cinemagoer, and so the magic of the silver screen had always held a certain mystique for me. He said sure, hop in.

I remember arriving at the camera department at the huge Denham Studios, which were controlled by Alexander Korda, where we'd pick up the film cans. The approach to the studio was something in itself. As you drew nearer the giant "London Films" sign stood out from the side of the stages like an imposing giant over the sleepy village. It was a different world, a magical world, and as I was an avid cinemagoer, I knew of many of the great films Korda had made and, of course, the famous ones at Denham: *Elephant Boy, The Drum* and *The Four Feathers,* to name but three. The film cans we were sent to collect weren't always ready, and so I'd kill a little time by having a nose around the studio and sometimes on a stage, to see what was shooting. I think it was then that the bug really bit. It's hard to describe, really, but I felt this was it—this is what I was truly destined for. Not the glamour of appearing in front of the camera, but working on films in some capacity behind the camera … or *with* it! As the weeks went by, I got to know the people in the camera department quite well and we'd have a chat over a cup of tea. But it was a conversation I overheard that really set things in motion. The guys were saying that "young John" had been called up, and so such-and-such a film had lost their clapperboy. My ears pricked up.

I thought I'd pop over the next day, Saturday, knowing they always worked, and have a word. I knocked on Bert Easey's door; he was the head of the camera department and a lovely chap. I said that I'd heard there was a vacancy for a clapperboy. We chatted for ten minutes or so, and he was asking me about my background and work at the labs. "Okay, come with me," he said. We walked down to Stage 3 and, I'll never forget, they were shooting *First of the Few* with Leslie Howard and David Niven, all about the invention of the Spitfire. Cracking stuff.

So there was I with my best collar and tie on, raincoat over my arm standing like a lemon watching Bert talking with the various camera people. They were looking over at me. One came over and spoke to me, and then another followed by the producer. "Okay, can you start now?" I explained that I had to give a week's notice at the film labs, but he was quite clear—if I couldn't report for work on Monday, then I wasn't to bother at all. Blimey, I thought, what am I going to do? I thought for a moment and very assertively said, "Right! I'll be here." With that, I trotted off to the station to go into Acton and to Olympic Film Labs.

I told them I was leaving. They said I couldn't. I was, by now, very determined that my career lay in film production, and not in processing ... although both would later be inextricably linked. I said I was sorry, but that was that; I was leaving.

Denham Beckons

Denham Studios was an amazing place, and one probably forever associated with the late Sir Alexander Korda. He was a flamboyant producer-director and film executive who started out as a director in Hungary. But because of the political upheaval in 1919, he had to leave Hungary and settled in Austria. In 1926 he went to Hollywood and stayed for four years and then, eventually, moved to London in 1931 with his brothers Zoltan (a director) and Vincent (an art director). He employed them both on many, many of his films. It was really through the U.K. introducing a "Quota Act" that Korda got started. It was ruled that to try and stop the Hollywood dominance of British screens, there should be a minimum number of British films made—a minimum quota. Thus came the "Quota Quickie" films, inexpensive and straightforward, often shot in just a few weeks. Korda formed London Films and made many of these, before then venturing into bigger productions, not least *The Private Life of Henry VIII*. It made him, and his backers, a fortune. A few more successes followed and it was agreed that Korda should build his own studios to continue his production program. Thus Denham Studios was built over 1935-36 and in May '36 the 193-acre site, encompassing seven sound stages, opened for business. It was the largest studio in Britain. Unfortunately, fortunes took a turn for the worse and Korda found himself in financial difficulties. That's when J. Arthur Rank stepped in and took control of the studio, though Korda remained very much *in situ*.

On the proverbial Monday morning, I reported to Denham Studios, picked up my clapperboard and started work.

You might be wondering what a clapper boy actually does. It's one of the lowlier positions within the camera team, but again gives a very good grounding as you're close to the action and can see everything going on. Essentially, it's a job which helps the labs (there they are again!) and editor identify the sequence of film. Each scene has a number, and there can be several "takes" of any particular one. The Clapper Boy numbers up his board with the scene and take, jumps in front of the camera once it is "rolling" and before the director calls "Action." He gives it a snap and gets out of the way. The snap is for the editor to get a sound synchronization—he can match the snap sound to seeing it on the clapperboard, and hence everything is in sync. Simple when you know how.

"What's your name, son?" the crew asked. "George," I replied, because my name is George Alan Hume, and I was always known as George.

"Not on this film you're not. The cameraman is George Perinal, the assistant is George Pollock, the prop man is George Francis...." They had five on the crew.

"What's your middle name?" he asked. I told him it was Alan. "Right, from now on you're Alan."

That's how my name changed instantly from George to Alan, and it's stuck ever since! Funny how things like that happen, isn't it?

I guess I was at Denham for about 14 months. I did all sorts of things from shooting first and second unit, to titles and special effects on the tank. It was a pretty broad and good grounding.

As I recalled, my first film was entitled *The First of the Few.* Thankfully, it became the first of many, but I digress. It starred Leslie Howard, David Niven, Rosamund John and a whole host of other great names and, indeed, heroes of mine. It was all about how, by the late 1920s, aircraft designer R.J. Mitchell feels he has achieved all he wants with his revolutionary mono planes winning trophy after trophy. But a holiday in Germany shortly after Hitler assumes power convinces him that it is vital to design a completely new type of fighter plane and that sooner or later Britain's very survival may depend on what he comes to call the Spitfire.

It was a terrific film and amazing story. Leslie Howard directed it too. It was his third film as director I believe, his first being the wonderful *Pygmalion* in 1938. He'd produced probably three times as many films and starred in almost 40, including *Gone with the Wind, In Which We Serve* and *The Scarlet Pimpernel.* Sadly, he died in 1943 when a plane he was traveling in was shot down by the Luftwaffe. It was upsettingly ironic he should die in this way having directed a film about the Spitfire.

I was the lowest of the low, so to say, on this film as clapper boy. I moved along on to other productions one after the other. Sadly, it's a bit of a blur nowadays as there were many films; it was the time of the British film industry's greatest output. I remember *Flemish Farm* and *Tawney Pipit,* both wartime-set films, as was the film where I had my first brush with David Lean; I did a bit of work on *In Which We Serve* out at Denham. I remember we filmed a lot on the tank at the studio, and it was absolutely filthy with gunk (representing a torpedoed destroyer) and I think the main fear amongst the actors was swallowing some of the water and coming down with some awful disease. More on David later. One of the other films that sticks in my mind—for all the right reasons—is *Thunder Rock.*

Thunder Rock was adapted from a play by Robert Audrey, by Jeffrey Dell and Bernard Miles. It was directed by Roy Boulting and produced by John Boulting—the Boulting Brothers, as they were famously known. Roy had directed a few other films before this one, and John produced. They then took turns and alternated their roles. Without doubt, they were the finest filmmakers of the day and made some amazing and powerful movies. I'm going to talk about them a little more if you don't mind as it's important I do so.

They were very much middle-class people, and had grown up as such at the seaside near Brighton. It was by pure luck that one day their nanny suggested instead of their three miles walk, as it was raining heavily, that they go to the cinema. They went to see *The Four Horsemen of the Apocalypse* and thus were captivated by the magic of cinema. From then on, the young twins knew this world was for them.

In their mid-twenties they embarked upon their first film, *Trunk Crime* (1939). There was no stopping them afterwards.

Thunder Rock was their third film and a very powerful one too. It was about an anti-fascist journalist in Canada (Michael Redgrave) failing in his political movement because of the greed and avarice of his fellow workers and the self-satisfaction of the public.

He chose to retire to an isolated lighthouse on Lake Michigan, in disgust with the world of the '30s. The lighthouse rock sustains a commemorative tablet to a group of European immigrants whose ship sank off-shore during a storm a century before.

As the weeks turn into months, the writer begins to imagine the ghosts of the dead names appearing before him, each telling their tale of sorrow, of escaping, of seeking a new life. In the end he decides he has no cause to complain, and that it is his duty to keep on fighting, even if only for the sake of the dead he has conjured up.

It was a great cast: Michael Redgrave, Barbara Mullen, James Mason, Finlay Currie, Miles Malleson, A.E. Matthews and many others. The lighting cameraman was a German named Mutz Greenbaum. He was a brilliant man, and a great-humored one too and I remember everyone loved working with him, me especially.

There is a particular scene in the film that you may know of. It is when we are aware that Redgrave's character is conjuring up the dead, so to say, in a dream-like sequence.

Roy wanted this "dream sequence" to differ from the rest of the film up until then. You see, the audience don't quite yet realize that it is all in the character's mind, and that dubiousness was something Roy wanted to play on. However, he felt he needed to differentiate the look of this scene somehow, and slightly, so as the audience would suspect that something is not quite right. Many discussions took place about maybe using filters, or dissolves, or altering the lighting. But neither Mutz nor Roy was totally happy.

It then came to Mutz. He had a brilliant idea, and one which he recalled was used some years earlier on a film he made in Germany. They tilted the floor on the set by about 15 degrees. But surely, you say, that would look a bit odd compared to scenes before now. True. But the genius in his thought was to put the camera on the tilted floor, flush.

So think about it, you had a tilted floor and a camera on that tilted floor. To all intents and purposes it was the same as before—the camera being perpendicular. So there was no visible difference. True, but Mutz said, "Think about how the actors react to the change in gravity."

He was right. You watch the film and whilst the set appears unchanged, in the dream sequence the actors walk very peculiarly—because of gravity, of course. It had the most wonderful effect. I learned so much from Mutz.

Then, my next little bit of luck came about. One of the focus pullers on a film was called-up to the forces (the War was still raging). There was a boy slightly ahead of me, and he was upgraded to focus puller for Denham Studios' output. In the event, he lasted two days! And so I was offered the chance to pull focus and that was my bit of luck. I have to admit to being very nervous, though.

I managed to get through my first film without being fired, and a few more too, including one at Ealing Studios before being called-up.

I know, I know. What's a focus puller, you're asking? It's a lot more technical than clapper boy, and involves you hands-on the camera and more often than not sitting underneath or to the side of it. Essentially, as there are different lenses for various applications, you have to know exactly how to turn each lens to achieve a certain focus at a certain point. Actors have marks to hit on the stage, usually a cross on the floor, and the focus puller is the one with the tape measure, measuring the distance between the mark and camera, so he knows what focus to pull when the actor hits the mark, ensuring a crystal clear image on film. Well, most of the time! It can be quite complicated in heavy scenes and required a lot of concentration.

As I mentioned, I then received the call-up. I joined the Navy, and served in the photographic unit. It was very interesting and I learned more about photography in the Navy than anywhere else. I wasn't involved in the film side, such as making training shorts, but rather as a stills photographer. It involved lots of aerial photography, making mosaics and maps, doing all sorts of ship recognition photographs ... right through to passport photos. You name it, I did it.

After the war, I was demobbed in 1946 and was told that they couldn't take me back at Denham as there was nothing doing. My last film had been at Ealing, so by law I was entitled to reinstatement there. They didn't particularly want me, but begrudgingly took me. It was a matter of weeks before Bert Easey called from Denham. He said he had a job if I wanted it. I was there the next Monday!

David Lean

Around this time, at Denham, there was a young director who was making a name for himself. He'd already co-directed *In Which We Serve* and had recently completed *Great Expectations*. He was, of course, David Lean. His next project was going to be made at Pinewood Studios. Both Pinewood and Denham were under the control of J. Arthur Rank at this time, and so switching between the two was not a problem. In fact, soon afterwards Denham closed and everything was transferred to Pinewood.

Alan (holding out measuring rule) pulls focus for David Lean on Oliver Twist.

For *Oliver Twist* they needed a focus puller, and I was put forward and duly accepted. That was an amazing experience. There was David Lean directing, Ronald Neame producing, Guy Green was lighting and Ossie Morris operating. I was on the film for quite a long time and struck up a good working relationship with them all. So much so, I went on to their next three films with them.

David Lean was an amazing director. He was so thorough and determined to achieve his vision, yet was very considerate, charming and kind. Funnily enough, he started out pulling focus and so appreciated it wasn't the easiest of jobs, and as such he was always very kind towards me.

I watched Guy Green avidly. He was one of the best in the business and I was determined to learn from him. I'd sit, between set-ups, behind the camera and follow everything he did. I was genuinely interested in photography and lighting and I think they saw that. Guy was without doubt one of the greatest black-and-white cameramen in the world. He knew how to light his leading ladies to greatest effect and he knew how to light locations and settings to create meaning. I think his greatest and most satisfying work was with David Lean. I was so fortunate to be there at this time. He went on to work as a freelance cameraman and made some terrific films, before himself turning his hand to directing. Perhaps his most evocative film was *The Angry Silence* produced by Richard Attenborough and Bryan Forbes; and starring Attenborough, Michael Craig and Bernard Lee. It was a tense drama about how a worker was "sent to Coventry" (ignored) by his fellow workers after he refused to join an unofficial strike. Guy's direction was superb, and he won some wonderful reviews.

III

Onwards and Upwards

David Lean, Anthony Havelock-Allan and Ronnie Neame had formed a company called Cineguild for their first feature, *This Happy Breed.* Cineguild in turn became part of J. Arthur Rank's Independent Producer's company. Others included Launder & Gilliat and Powell & Pressberger. They were pretty much left alone to make films they wanted to make, and Rank financed them.

Cineguild went on to *Brief Encounter* and *Great Expectations.* The relationship between Ronnie and David was at best tense. David had little time for producers, other than for their raising money, and with his increasing bankability and power as a director, the relationship deteriorated further. The rows were frequent, and yet they remained the greatest of friends underneath. It was a few years before the relationship, and company, would crumble.

Meanwhile, David's masterpiece was in the making. *Oliver Twist* was nothing short of extraordinary filmmaking. The opening sequence is particularly chilling and gripping, as was David's intention, with Josephine Stuart staggering to the workhouse to give birth to Oliver. In fact, we re-shot the first take as he thought Guy Green's photography "too romantic," with clouds swirling in the sky and a storm brewing. The storm was intensified, and it remains one of the most impressive scenes in cinema history.

John Howard Davies was cast as the young Oliver, but by far the most inspired piece of casting—and there was already Robert Newton and Kay Walsh—was Alec Guinness as Fagin. Alec had appeared in *Great Expectations* and approached David about the part of Fagin. I think it would be fair to say David laughed him out of his office. Alec begged David to give him a test, and the director agreed—if only for old times' sake. Alec laid down one condition—that David would not attempt to catch a glimpse of him before he was ready to walk on the set. He agreed. With the assistance of make up genius Stuart Freeborn, Alec transformed himself into Fagin. He walked onto the set and, without having to say a word, he was awarded the part.

The film was a runaway success.

David went off for a well-deserved holiday, and Ronnie Neame turned his hand to directing his first film, *Take My Life*. After this one, he seemed confident enough to secure a second vehicle and, with J. Arthur Rank suggesting a love story would suit the distribution network, Ronnie settled on *The Passionate Friends,* based on H G Wells' novel. Eric Ambler wrote the screenplay and a cast including Claude Rains, Marius Goring and Ann Todd was assembled. The film started shooting but it was soon very apparent that Ronnie was losing his confidence. After three days, shooting was halted.

The rushes proved disappointing. In the event, David was asked to replace Ronnie Neame as the director, but Ronnie remained as producer. David subsequently replaced Goring with Trevor Howard.

Guy Green's photography was quite different on this film to the last we had worked on together. The whole look of the film was far removed from *Oliver Twist* in that this was very stylish and romantically photographed, and great care was taken with the close-ups of Ann Todd. To create the right mood and atmosphere, David suggested the use of a pianist who would play between scenes and set-ups.

David was very technical, and thought of everything as an editor would. He'd often talk to Ossie Morris about how many frames he wanted of such-and-such a scene, and how he wanted him to pan here, and freeze there. It was quite something for an avid beginner to watch.

Independent Frame

At this time there was a process called Independent Frame, which I will come to in some more detail, involving rear and front projection as a substitute for location shooting. The pressure was on David to use it for some sequences in the film, but he steadfastly refused and insisted on traveling to the locations, including the Swiss Alps. Such was the power he was garnering.

Although the film cannot be categorized as a classic, it has its merits and stands up pretty well. I think David Lean said it was "almost very good." I'd agree. It was certainly lovingly photographed by Guy Green.

I've mentioned Independent Frame, and it certainly deserves more coverage. Although in fact it turned out to be a disaster in itself, the innovations and technology development it brought about are still being used today. Independent Frame (IF) was a technical project in which Rank invested heavily. As far back as 1944, plans were hatched for the project. David Rawnsley (the art director on *In Which We* Serve) was the leading force behind IF, which was said to be set to "revolutionize filmmaking" primarily by shortening film schedules and saving money on set constructions and location shooting.

The idea appealed to Rank, especially in light of the ever-increasing and extravagant excesses of some producers and their productions, because it offered an inexpensive production process and, moreover, a very welcome means of supplying and keeping busy his distribution and cinema companies. Rawnsley's idea stemmed from working on *49th Parallel* where he had shot a multitude of background plates (the location shots that would be projected onto screens in the studio, in front or behind artistes, to give the impression of artistes actually being there). He thought that, by taking the process a little further in terms of the available technology and craftsmanship, then it should be possible to combine projection with matte effects, split screens, etc.—all the processes used to accomplish certain shots and sequences in special effects—into one great project: Independent Frame.

Additionally, Rawnsley—who became head of the Rank Research Department—knew that during the War, sound stage space was at a premium. During a typical production, two out of three stages would be in use. For every stage on which shooting was taking place, another stage would have carpenters and technicians building or pulling down sets. What if, he thought, instead of building a set on the stage and then moving the unit in to shoot, the unit could stay on the stage and different sets moved in and out to them? Not only would it increase stage capacity, it would provide an inexpensive way of filming.

Fred Pelton of MGM had worked in Hollywood on this idea of never building sets on the actual stage, but he ended up by needing elaborate machinery, with miniature railway lines and hydraulic lifts, to move them into position. Rawnsley decided that sets would need to be small, and so he designed small creak-proof rostrums, adjustable in height and angle, which could be wheeled in and out, and put together on the stage to produce sets of any size. And so sets and backdrops would be wheeled in and out of the stages, on these Vickers rostrums, and with the use of specially modified cameras all would combine to quicken the filmmaking process. Gone would be the lengthy construction times and changing of sets and stages and in would come a factory "conveyor belt" system. The sets were wheeled in; the artistes followed, rehearsed and then shot the scene. Then they'd move to another stage whilst the sets on the first were being wheeled out and replaced, to shoot further scenes and so the process continued. The theory sounded simple and good.

Rawnsley decided that the back projection screen itself must be made mobile too. He designed a mobile lighting platform, electrically operated, which could hold up to six lamps. It would be no good, of course, wheeling in a back projection screen, the ready-made set and the lighting platform, if an enormous amount of time then had to be taken up deciding exactly where they had to go, while the actors stood around waiting. Therefore, the whole stage was divided up into squares, and each had a number. Squares were then marked up, on instruction from the Art Director, on where the cameras had to be placed—otherwise the shot wouldn't fill the screen properly. The director had to plan his angles well in advance, with an exactly accurate shooting script. We used to go on the floor and say, "We're shooting scene 28"; the reply would come back, "That's square 34 shooting towards square 19 and you'll be on the screen in such-and-such a position." It never really worked though, as we were often off the screen or that part of set we wanted.

Rawnsley borrowed planning methods evolved by Disney, and also studied the work of the BBC at Alexandra Palace. He was impressed by the thoughts of using TV cameras in filmmaking, allowing the director to see, at any moment of shooting, exactly what would appear on screen, instead of waiting for rushes to be processed.

There would, of course, be a massive collection or "library" of backgrounds, which would be an added bonus as again, time could be saved in constructing these on other productions which they might lend themselves to.

The first IF film made at Pinewood was *Warning to Wantons*. Movement was heavily restricted on these sets and the projection techniques were never really totally satisfactory as it was a frustrating process synching the projector shutter frequency with that of the camera filming the action, and actors often had a "glow" around them in these scenes. The process was later modified and perfected by Charles Staffell, who won an Oscar for his work in the projection process—the first, and only, one awarded for technical work such as this.

However, it wouldn't be fair to blame the demise of IF on its raw technology—technology that was later refined and is still in use today. But rather after Rank invested £600,000 in the venture, there was a problem facing the British film Industry and his studios.. It wasn't about how to save studio space with a decline in production, there was a problem of keeping them in use.

At the same time, the "traveling matte" process evolved at Pinewood, and it largely superseded the back projection techniques developed thus far. With traveling matte, instead of photographing actors against a background plate together, the background and actors were photographed separately—the actors in a specially filtered yellow light against a particular shade of blue curtain—and the two are married in the final print. This process has many advantages over back projection, not least the fact the background can be enlarged indefinitely, whereas with back projection a 30-foot screen was really the biggest one could employ in order to match the light on the background with that on the actors in the foreground. With back projection it was also sometimes difficult to get the screen and the actors in sharp focus at the same time.

Sadly, David Rawnsley's work in films was cut short by an illness which took him to the South of France.

Butterflies

Ralph Thomas and Betty Box were names which later became synonymous with British film.

Betty was the producer and Ralph the director. Betty started out in the business with her older brother Sydney, as his assistant, and soon progressed to producing herself. Ralph was an accomplished editor and was described as "natural" director, an observation I would very much agree with. The pleasure of working with directors who had previously been editors (I think a majority of directors I worked with came from the cutting rooms) was that they knew exactly what they needed to film and how best to achieve tension, drama and comedy. They could physically "cut" the film in their minds as they shot it.

Betty and Ralph joined forces and, with their own company, the legend "A Betty Box-Ralph Thomas Production," graced their films together. That they should come together and work in a partnership that lasted nearly 30 years says a lot about them. They were lovely people and went on to make both amusing, touching and important films. My first brush with them came with *The Clouded Yellow* (which is the name of a butterfly—and central to the murder mystery plot). It was their first feature together, in fact, and as with any film, the financing proved tricky but perhaps more so than we, on the film, realized. We'd started production and some of the money hadn't arrived. Unbeknown to us, up on location in the Lake District, Betty and her husband Peter Rogers (of whom more later) mortgaged their house in the London suburbs to keep the film going.

Mercifully, the rest of the money eventually arrived, and the film was a great financial success! And not one of us even got a hint of any financial problems—Betty was very wise. Keep the production going and don't worry the crew unnecessarily!

Back with Lean

David Lean moved on to his next project, and I was asked to join him. It was *Madeleine* and was based on the 1850s murder case, when Madeleine Smith was put on trial for the suspected murder of her lover. Meanwhile, on a neighboring stage Ronnie Neame was directing *The Golden Salamander.*

I remember it being a particularly long schedule. There was an electrician's strike halfway through, which saw the picture put on hold. All in all, it took 21 weeks from start to finish. Around this time, Rank's Managing Director, John Davis, was closely scrutinizing film output. The Organization was losing money and running a large overdraft, and he was keen to cut costs. Redundancies resulted, production programs halted and Independent Producers was wound-up as a company. Gone was the creative freedom and seemingly limitless supply of funds of the producers within the group, and Cineguild fell apart.

It was a very quiet time in the British film Industry, and very depressing. I know David was keen to stay with Rank, but the proposed budget on his next film proved too high for them. So, like many of his contemporaries, he left for Shepperton to join Alexander Korda.

Korda was, in a way, the nearest thing we ever had to a "mogul" in the sense of the American producers. He was flamboyant, a visionary and had overcome several bankruptcies. When he was struggling in the early 1940s, Rank was scaling new heights. Now the tables were reversed, and Korda—although in his latter years—embarked upon ambitious films once again, and with a new base (for Rank had taken over Denham) at Shepperton Studios in Middlesex. Whilst perhaps Shepperton wasn't as superior as Denham had been, it was studio with an independent spirit, and I feel it was inevitable that Korda should have moved there.

Stand and Deliver

I remember one of the next films I worked on, as focus puller, was a big American adventure called *Dick Turpin's Ride.* It starred Louis Hayward. As I say it was American, but they came to England for some location work, and the lighting cameraman they used for these sequences was Harry Waxman. The director, Ralph Murphy, I don't remember much about, but I do remember the producer, Harry Joe Brown. A typical loud-mouthed, cigar-puffing Hollywood mogul type who had a liking for a loud-hailer.

He was a bit of a brute to put it mildly, but he was very professional in achieving the final result and cared about making a good film (his career, as producer and director, went back to the early 1920s and silent films). This was a Columbia production and I believe one of their early productions in the UK. I think that Harry (who was actually a big cheese within Columbia) was testing us out to a certain degree, as the view of us British was a tea-drinking mob who weren't very professional. Well after we completed this film, Columbia made a whole lot more over here!

I recall we had a few locations on the film, and one was out at Ashridge Park, I guess about 30 minutes drive. The orders were given to the crew assemble at Pinewood at 7:30 A.M. sharp in order we could be at the location, on the bus, at 8:15 A.M. This was back in the days where traffic congestion wasn't an issue. Dutifully, we all turned up and the bus was ready to depart when one of the carpenters suddenly realized he'd left some tools in his workshop in the studio. He dashed off to collect them, but held us all up by a good ten minutes I'd say. Anyway, once we were all back on board, we left for the location. As we pulled up at the front gate at 8:25 A.M., Harry was there with his Rolls-Royce, and was not looking very happy.

Peter Manley, the second Assistant Director, whose job it was to get everyone there on time, went across to apologize. He never made any excuses, as Peter is far too professional for that. But Harry was furious that we'd wasted ten minutes of his day, and he had every right to be so. We were due back at the location the next day and as we returned home that night, Peter said to everyone on the bus that he expected all the crew to be on board and ready to leave at 7:15 the next morning or they'd be left behind. You know, at 7:15 we were leaving the studio with everyone and every tool on board!

On another location, a shot went wrong, the horse and carriage didn't quite do as it was expected—these things happen. One of the assistants shouted "Whoa, whoa, whoa." Harry Joe Brown was furious. "Who the fuck shouted *whoa*? *I'm* the only one here who shouts *whoa*. When I shout *whoa* you *whoa*, and not until then."

We knew our place.

Next, we were setting up a shot near a cottage and two little old ladies who lived there were taking a great interest and were outside leaning on the gate watching. Harry said to the assistant director Phil Shipway "would you get those ladies out of here, they're in shot." So off the young guy went to talk to them, and when I say talk he did talk. We all stood there watching them chat away, casting occasional glances in our direction. About ten minutes later, he came back. "What took you so long?" snapped Harry. Cool as a cucumber, Phil turned and said, "Oh, those ladies wanted to know who the noisy bastard with the loud-hailer was." Harry went red, but did crack a laugh in the end.

The thing that most impressed me with Harry was his organizational skills. He'd made a lot of Western films back in Hollywood, so was quite at home with horses, chases and so on and knew how to handle them, and get the best shots to create a tension. We were setting up a shot of Dick Turpin, on horseback, being chased by the authorities (in a horse-drawn carriage). Harry paced out the shot and said, "Put the camera here." X marked the spot. He then said, "I want the carriage to be such-and-such a distance behind Turpin's horse." The result was such that Turpin's horse came into view, racing towards our camera, and just as he reached the camera (our edge of frame), in the distance the carriage came into view. It was timed perfectly. "Right," said Harry, "turn the camera around 180 degrees." We did.

He then did the same sequence, with the same distances, but shooting in the opposite direction. So in came Turpin's horse from behind us running past and just as he reached the edge of the frame, in came the carriage. The timing was perfect, and in one set-up we'd achieved our shot plus a shot from behind the horses, giving us some excellent cutaway material. It was fast, furious and perfect!

Although only here a few weeks, Harry actually admitted to like working with us Brits, and he threw a little drinks party for us all at Pinewood. It was there when Harry was saying how professional we all were that Phil Shipway chirped up, "Yes, but I bet you go back and tell them all a different story, and how we stop for tea every ten minutes. You Americans always do."

Harry, quite taken aback, assured us that it wasn't the case. He really did think us terrific and very professional and he had tears in his eyes as he waved goodbye. Phil was unconvinced. However, a few weeks later a large envelope arrived at the studio, addressed to Phil. He opened it to discover a copy of *Variety* magazine. And inside Harry Joe Brown spoke about filming in the UK and said that he felt us the most professional and fun crew he'd ever worked with. Phil was flabbergasted. Not only was Harry genuine, he'd gone to the trouble of phoning up *Variety* and then to the trouble of sending us a copy.

Whilst I still stand by saying he was an abrupt, rude man—he was—I do admire him!

After this picture, I found work had all but dried up and, facing the harsh reality of my financial status, took a job in a local timber yard. Thankfully it wasn't for too long as things started to pick up again and I was back.

Africa

When I heard about *Hotel Sahara*, a North African–set film, I thought my luck was in for a nice hot sojourn in the sun. No such luck,

I'm afraid, as the hottest we got was under the large brute lamps at Pinewood! "Never mind, it's a job," I thought.

It was a lovely little comedy, actually, with Peter Ustinov playing a hotel owner in the aforementioned Sahara, and being an adept businessman he changed loyalties to suit his occupiers. So if a German party arrived, up went the German flag. If a French party, up went the French flag and so on.

Peter was a terrific character to have on set, and very, very funny. I remember one day between set-ups he was eating a delicious cream doughnut and a little bit of cream fell down onto his sandal. Without hesitation—and in character—he said to me, "My goodness, it's a good job there aren't any tsetse flies around or they'd be on me like a shot with that on my foot."

It seemed that I had developed a bit of a reputation on set, as still being a pretty fast "loader." During my days as clapper loader, one of my tasks was to change the film magazine on the camera. I wouldn't say it's particularly difficult or complicated, but there is a knack to doing it just right. Anyway, unbeknownst to me, the production team had a bet and decided to ask me to change a magazine whilst timing me. It took ten seconds flat. A pretty decent achievement if I do say so myself!

Wilkie

I next linked up with a great cinematographer called Wilkie Cooper and embarked upon the most important era of my career to date. We first worked on *Pickwick Papers* with James Haytor, when I was a focus puller, but on the second film *Our Girl Friday,* he promoted me to camera operator. I guess he saw a bit of potential in this then-young chap!

The film was quite an exotic one. We all went out to Majorca to film; the director was a chap named Noel Langley, who'd also written the script. I think it was by virtue of having penned the piece that he got the director's job. It certainly wasn't on the merit of his directing skills, let me tell you. He was pretty useless, in fact, and it meant Wilkie and I had to do that much more.

Young Joan Collins, the star, was being hailed as the next Elizabeth Taylor. George Cole, Robertson Hare and Kenneth More co-starred in the tale of four shipwrecked folks on an island. It could be described as a coy sex comedy, I suppose. Not really notable amongst the great films of all time, but it was quite memorable for me and indeed a great location to start my career as an operator!

Peter Ellenshaw

But I'm jumping ahead of myself here. You see, after *Pickwick Papers* and before Wilkie gave me a break as an operator, I teamed up with a very talented artist by the name of Peter Ellenshaw for 18 months or so. That was a very important period in my career, and one in which I learned a tremendous amount about camerawork.

I had, until then, been a focus puller but I then heard of how Peter was starting a matte department at Denham for Walt Disney and how he needed a camera technician. Matte painting, as I touched upon earlier, was when picture painted on glass is combined with live-action or miniature elements to create an environment. I wonder if you knew that most famous shots in film history were largely created using traditional or digital matte paintings—Tara from *Gone with the Wind*, the Emerald City in *The Wizard of Oz, Citizen Kane*'s Xanadu, *King Kong*'s Skull Island, versions of Imperial Rome in both *Ben Hur* and *Gladiator*, Bodega Bay in Hitchcock's *The Birds*, large portions of the original *Star Wars* films? Well, they were. Of course, the digital side of matte work is a relatively new advancement, whereas my grounding was very much in the traditional paint-and-glass technology.

Peter was a brilliant artist and, aside from his film work, painted many great landscapes and country scenes. In fact, at home I have several of his paintings in my lounge. He was born in 1913 in Essex and as a young man he met the British portrait painter W. Percy Day, O.B.E. (Pop Day), who subsequently married Peter's mother. Day was instrumental in developing the highly demanding technique of matte painting. Peter convinced Day to hire him as his assistant, and, for the next seven years, the two artists worked closely together on such epics as *Things to Come, Rembrandt, The Four Feathers, The Drum* and *The Thief of Baghdad.*

During World War II, Peter served as a pilot in the Royal Air Force. After the war, he set up his own studio and struck out on his own working as a matte artist in Rome on *Quo Vadis* and painting the ships in *Captain Hornblower R.N.* By 1948, the increasing expense of making films in Hollywood led Walt Disney to England for the production of four live-action adventure films (*Treasure Island, The Story of Robin Hood, The Sword and The Rose* and *Rob Roy*). When Disney met Peter and became acquainted with his work, his response was immediate and enthusiastic. Here was the man who could recreate in Disney's films the historical England of centuries past and, through matte painting, save the cost of many difficult location shots.

We were based at Denham Studios, as I mentioned, in the old stables and I guess I worked pretty solidly with Peter for 18 months. The whole technique of filming using matte painting is quite labor-intensive and time-consuming. We would shoot the original scene (in Technicolor) and send it off to be processed. Then we would get the separation masters; red, blue and cyan.

Peter would "paint in" what was to be the top of the scene, be it a sky, a castle on a hill or whatever, on a glass sheet. Using the original negatives, we would then begin the process of exposing the original piece of the film. We'd black out the bottom part of the sequence (which was the live-action captured part) whilst lighting the top part (the matte painting) and run the film through and expose that top part of the negative. It was quite a long process of exposure and color correction as each color strip would have to be exposed individually.

We were very, very careful not to slip up (as a mistake on any one of the passes of film would mean back to square one) but on one occasion the chap loading the magazine, loaded it the wrong way around. We didn't realize it until many hours later and after many rewinds of the film through the camera!

We worked on these three Disney films together in England before, in 1953, Disney asked Ellenshaw to work with him on *20,000 Leagues Under the Sea* in Hollywood. Peter jumped at the chance and, after sell-

Loser Takes All cinema release poster.

ing his home in England, he moved to the United States with his wife and son, Harrison. In all, Peter was involved in 34 films for Walt Disney Productions between 1947 and 1979. Disney encouraged and challenged Peter constantly to exceed his previous accomplishments. The harmonious relationship between the two proved highly productive professionally and deeply gratifying personally. Peter maintained his identity as a traditional landscape artist during his Disney years and always found time evenings and weekends to work on his own canvases.

In 1979, the American film Institute honored Peter with a retrospective exhibition of his work that was shown at the Museum of Modern Art, New York; the American film Institute, Washington, D.C.; the film Institute, Chicago; and the Academy of Motion Picture Arts and Sciences Los Angeles. The exhibition included paintings, production designs (including advance sketches from *The Black Hole*) and mattes from his 45-year career in motion pictures. Also included were Peter's paintings of the Himalayan mountains that helped win an Oscar for Best Color Cinematography for *Black Narcissus* (1947) and his painting of the Edwardian skyline of London that earned him a special effects Oscar for *Mary Poppins* (1964).

In 1993, Peter was named a Disney Legend.

Back with Wilkie

As mentioned, I then began operating on films for Wilkie Cooper; the next few included *Dance Little Lady* for director Val Guest, *Portrait of Alison* with Terry Moore and *The End of the Affair* with Van Johnson, Deborah Kerr, Peter Cushing and John Mills, directed by Edward Dmytryk.

Dmytryk was an interesting chap. The son of Ukrainian immigrants, he grew up in San Francisco. He found work as a studio messenger when he was 15, but was outstanding student in physics and mathematics, gaining a scholarship to the California Institute of Technology. However, he dropped out after one year to return to movies, eventually working his way up from film editor to director. By the late 1940s he was considered one of Hollywood's rising young directing talents, but his career was interrupted by the activities of the "House Un-American Activities Committee," and he became one of the blacklisted "Hollywood 10" in the '50s following his brief membership of the Communist Party. After a stint in jail, he decided to cooperate and renounce Communism. Although he always claimed he believed he had done the right thing, with no regrets, many in Hollywood never forgave him, and his action overshadowed his career the rest of his life. He made films such as *Shalako, Bluebeard* and *The Human Factor* before turning to teaching.

The film I did with him, in 1955, was—as mentioned—*The End of the Affair*, based on the Graham Greene story (it was re-made a few years back with Ralph Fiennes and Julianne Moore). Then a film I did with Wilkie, *The Green Man*, filmed over at Shepperton, resulted in my being offered a contract as camera operator at the studio. All the best guys were ending up there!

Films like the wonderfully *Geordie* with Alastair Sim, Bill Travers and Miles Malleson (directed by Frank Launder), director Ken Annakin's comedy *Three Men in a Boat* with David Tomlinson, Jimmy Edwards and Shirley Eaton, *The Green Man* directed by Bob Day and again starring Alastair Sim, and *Loser Takes All*, another Graham Greene story directed by Ken Annakin followed. It was an amazing period as I virtually moved from film to film, with such great directors and artists. It was an apprenticeship I couldn't have dreamt of! They all presented their own challenges, and certainly *Three Men in a Boat* was a tricky film as we had adverse weather conditions, and problems with the water. Achieving "shooting conditions" often involved a lot of hanging around and improvising. But with each challenge, we found a solution and that hands-on learning is really invaluable. They can't teach you it at film school.

Paul Young plays the young Geordie McTaggart.

Top: Bill Travers plays the older wee Geordie McTaggart opposite Alastair Sim as the Laird. *Bottom:* Alastair Sim receives disturbing news in *The Green Man.*

George Cole and Alastair Sim in *The Green Man.*

Boating

With *Three Men in a Boat* I remember one little funny incident which I'll share with you. There was a sequence involving three characters in a boat punting across a river. It proved tricky punting this boat, and so we decided we'd set up a line across the river to which the boat could be hooked and props could pull it across, out of the camera's view. It took about two hours to get this rigged up. We were into the last rehearsal and along came the production manager up river in his speedboat, cutting straight across (and straight through) the line and off our boat drifted down river. It took a good hour to get sorted!

Another day we were filming the Henley Regatta. All along the river bank were piles that have been driven in all along and we had a long rope running between them to which lots of boats and punts were tied. It was all setting the scene. Then came all the extras in their period costumes. The assistant director, Peter Bolton, was called over by Ken Annakin. Ken said "Peter, we've been here two hours setting this scene and are still not there yet. Why don't we ask these people to get in the extra boats that need to be out there, and row out to tie themselves up." So Peter made an announcement to all those extras who felt capable of handling a boat to get in and row out. With that, everyone got in to a boat. Three old ladies in one, two chaps in another and so on. After about 30 minutes there was chaos: The main rope that linked all the (unmanned) boats along the bank, and the whole lot of boats started moving down river. Two hours later, the people in the boats were towing the unmanned boats back to position. A whole morning passed and we never shot a bloody foot of film.

Shepperton itself was much more of an "independents" studio. Denham and Pinewood had been dominated by London films and Rank's own output, and I guess there was a bit of a "club" feeling to it all. If you fitted in, well and good. Shepperton meanwhile, as I've already mentioned, had a much more independent spirit. Its most famous film was actually of this time: *The Third Man*, arguably Orson Welles' best film. The studio had a lot going for it—including lucky me!

I next signed up for a little portmanteau film called *The Extra Day* directed by Bill Fairchild and with a good cast including Richard Base-

Bryan Forbes (Harry) takes a moment to relax before his director calls for an *Extra Day* on set, after the last day rushes go missing!

Laurence Naismith (as Kurt Vorn) in *The Extra Day.*

heart, Sid James, George Baker, Laurence Naismith, Beryl Reid and a lovely young French actress named Simone Simon. I think we did a little bit of filming out at Beaconsfield (which I'll discuss more in a moment) and it was quite amusing actually as the film was all about making a film! On the last day of shooting, the film cans were taken to the labs for processing, and one rolled off the back of the van and was lost—necessitating an extra day of filming. Hence the title. But perish that thought!

Beaconsfield

In 1957, I was asked to go over to Beaconsfield Studios again, to join a production called *Vicious Circle*. Little did I know that it would effectively change my life.

Beaconsfield Studios was a fairly small set-up in the west London town, which was run by the Box family—Sydney, Muriel, Betty and her husband Peter Rogers. Sydney and Muriel had previously run Gainsborough Studios in Islington and Shepherds Bush, but when John Davis' hatchet fell on that division of the Rank Organization, they moved out to Beaconsfield where they had purchased the studio as a family concern. It's still there, and is in fact home to the National Film and Television School.

The studio, one of our smaller ones, was opened in 1922 by producer George Clark. It was reported that he wanted to escape the London smog whilst remaining close to a good rail link, and having country locations for outdoor filming of his comedy two-reelers. There was only one stage, a modest 120 feet x 60 feet. Three years later, though, times were hard and Clark was forced to close operations at the studio. It was two years later, anticipating the demand for studio space to produce "Quota Quickie" films, that British Lion acquired the studio. Modernization was undertaken and a number of Edgar Wallace novels were put into production. Significantly, whilst it is acknowledged that Hitchcock's *Blackmail* was Britain's first film to feature sound, the first all-talkie picture was actually 1929's *The Clue of the New Pin,* which was made by British Lion at Beaconsfield.

Sadly, in 1932 British Lion fell into financial difficulties and struggled to survive, but then Gaumont-Gainsborough made good use of the facility and kept the cameras turning over. Great names were at work including producer Michael Balcon, actors Gracie fields, Ann Todd, Jessie Matthews, Sophie Tucker and Florence Desmond. In mid–1937 Herbert Wilcox hired the studio for a number of films, including *The Return of the Frog,* an Edgar Wallace story. But when World War II broke out, the studio was requisitioned by the Ministry of Works for Rotax Limited, who manufactured magnetos for aircraft engines.

In 1947, British Lion controlled Beaconsfield, Shepperton and Worton Hall studios. They negotiated the sale of these studios to Alexander Korda. The independent spirit was back in control of not only one, but three UK studios having lost his beloved Denham a short time earlier.

After spending a few years at Pinewood during the War, the Crown film Unit invested £146,000 in Beaconsfield Studios and produced 75 films per year for the Ministry of Information until it was disbanded in 1951-52.

Michael Balcon then marked his return to the studio as chairman of Group 3 with a brief to develop new talent. Their films included *Miss Robin Hood* with Margaret Rutherford, James Robertson Justice and Sid James; *The Brave Don't Cry*; *The Oracle* with Robert Beatty, Virginia McKenna and Michael Medwin; a comedy called *Make Me an Offer* starring Peter Finch and Adrienne Corri; *The Blue Peter* with Kieron Moore and Greta Gynt; and *The Love Match,* a comedy with Arthur Askey, Thora Hird and Shirley Eaton.

Peter and Gerry

A few years later, the studio was taken over by the Box family and, significantly for me, Peter Rogers (a Box-in-law by marriage you might say) was producing a number of modest little films there; the one he asked me to join was the aforementioned *Vicious Circle,* based on a TV serial called *The Brass Candlestick*—a bit of a whodunit-type show. It had been adapted for this feature film by its writer Francis Durbridge and Peter had lined up John Mills, Derek Farr, Noelle Middleton, Roland Culver, Wilfrid Hyde White, Mervyn Johns, Lionel Jeffries … the list goes on, a real top-notch cast. Gerald Thomas was drafted in to direct. It was an interesting set-up with Peter and Gerald actually. Peter started off in life as a writer, moved into journalism and then was approached to work in the film business first by J Arthur Rank and then by Sydney Box. Peter married Sydney's sister Betty Box—a prolific producer in her own right—and later teamed up with Gerald, who was originally an editor for Betty and her director (and Gerald's brother) Ralph Thomas. A bit confusing, I know, but it was all one big family. Their first project was a children's film called *Circus Friends,* all about two circus children and their dog attempting to retrieve the circus pony, which had been given to a farmer in payment of a debt. It marked the start of their life-long partnership.

I worked on a couple of other films at Beaconsfield with Peter and Gerald including *Time Lock* in which Sean Connery debuted as a lowly blow torch operator, and the Tommy Steele starrer *The Duke Wore Jeans.* I was under a "handshake" contract at this time—lasting ten years in fact—and then talk started about an Army-set comedy. Meanwhile, Roger Moore had moved into the studio with the *Ivanhoe* TV series, and Peter found himself pushed out of his own studio, as there was no room! So he moved to Pinewood with what was to become *Carry On Sergeant.* The rest, as they say, is history.

IV

Carrying On

Carry On Sergeant was, quite unbeknown to any of us, to be the first of 31 in a series that spanned four decades in the cinema, and become phenomenally successful on TV too.

Carry On Sergeant was really the result of Peter seeing some potential in R.F. Delderfield's treatment of *The Bull Boys,* about the enforced enrollment into the army of ballet dancers. Peter got his scriptwriter Norman Hudis to work on it, adding a few touches of his own, and the ballet dancers replaced by a newly married couple desperately trying to consummate their union. The budget—through Anglo Amalgamated—was a pretty modest £75,000 and a shooting schedule of six five-day weeks.

So, on March 24 1958, the cameras rolled on the first *Carry On* film, at our location—Guildford Army Barracks. As far as we were concerned, it was just a one-off film with no pretensions of being anything else, let alone the catalyst for 30 more!

It was an ensemble cast from TV, radio and theater. There was Kenneth Williams, Kenneth Connor, Charles Hawtrey, Hattie Jacques, Bill Owen, Bob Monkhouse and, as the Sergeant himself, TV's *Doctor Who* William Hartnell. He was bloody good actually; he must have been in the Army as he had his character off to a tee and was quite believable to say the least—I certainly didn't cross his path!

After a week or two at Guildford—and they chose Guildford because it was within reasonable driving distance of the studio—it was back to

Opposite top: **Bob Monkhouse shows his felow recruits how it is(n't) done, with a little verbal encouragement from William Hartnell.** ***Bottom:*** **Charles Hawtrey lands right in it, during the training course in** ***Carry On Sergeant.***

Kenneth Connor shows he just isn't army material!

Pinewood. I think we finished at around about 4 P.M. and had a drink at the end of the picture. There was no overtime of any sort, unless we needed night shooting, and they got to the point of even locking the stages at lunchtime so as to prevent the propmen and the like from claiming overtime. It was all very strictly scheduled and budgeted and every penny was counted.

Of course, I was under contract—although on a handshake rather than signing anything—so to a certain extent I had to get on with it for a weekly fee, but to be honest there was such a wonderful, atmosphere on set I used to look forward to Monday mornings coming around and going back to work! It wasn't work really, it was great fun. When I wasn't working for Peter and Gerald, they used to "rent" me out and did very well actually, as they'd always tend to increase my fee (which they got)! Mind you, they always saw me okay for a few extra pounds in such cases.

Sequels

Next up, following the great success of the first film, was *Carry On Nurse*. I think that was the one that really launched the series in America. Shirley Eaton was in that one, and boy did she steal the show. So beautiful. It was a big hit in Australia too, and I remember someone saying that it ran in one cinema for a year. The formula remained the same though; the same team—albeit a slight change in cast—in front and behind the camera, the same schedule and the same studio. It was like a big family reunion! But the distributors wanted more still, and so Peter obliged. Up came *Teacher* in 1959, with Ted Ray guest starring. The next film saw an actor who had achieved some success in films as a supporting character (and as Tony Hancock's mate Sid in *Hancock's Half Hour* TV show) join the team. He was, of course, Sid James and his distinctive "filthy" laugh became infamously associated with the films.

Actually, the films were becoming funnier—both in scripting and

Charles Hawtrey, Kenneth Williams, Bernard Cribbins and Barbara Windsor are the cream of Britain's spy network, well almost, in *Carry On Spying.*

making. It was quite ridiculous but I used to have to stuff a handkerchief in my mouth, or walk away from the camera. I'm a terrific giggler and they really got me started! I remember that Gerry used to damn well start giggling in my ear at the side of the camera just to start me off. On one occasion, and a few films on, we were doing some night shooting on *Spying* in what was the prop building at Pinewood. It was supposed to be some sort of dockside building I think, where Kenny Connor and the others were to break in by climbing through a window. There they were, creeping around, and they knocked a couple of boxes over—boxes full of inflated balloons if you please. It was ludicrous and absolutely hilarious to watch. I couldn't bear it and had to dash behind one of the set walls with a hanky in my mouth. There I came face to face with Gerry Thomas with his hands over his face and we both burst out laughing!

In between takes, of course, I was really at my busiest. Cameras had to be moved, lights changed, marks chalked up and focus measured … all that sort of stuff, and so the crew is pretty damn busy. Meanwhile,

Sid James makes his *Carry On* debut, with Hattie Jacques in *Carry On Constable.*

Sharing a moment of tenderness, Sid James and Hattie Jacques in *Carry On Constable.*

the cast go off to a corner with their script and sit there laughing their heads off at what is to come. I could hardly bear it. I guess comedy isn't the best genre for a giggler like me to work in!

But back to *Constable* and the gang. I had worked with Sid James before, and so knew him quite well and he fitted in perfectly. It was an instant chemistry. Someone else who was drafted in again, after *Teacher*, was Leslie Phillips. He's just the same on screen and off, a really lovely guy. There was, of course, the famous scene where Leslie, Kenny Williams and Kenny Connor had to make a dash, in the nude, across the cell block where Joan Hickson and Joan Sims looked on. They had to do it in the buff too, though I think the stage was warmed up to take any chill off the air for obvious reasons!

Constable, as one would expect, called for scenes of the bobbies on the beat. So it was a location picture at last? Well, not quite. We ventured as far as Windsor (which was really like an extra stage, as we used it so much later on) and the bulk of the street sequences were shot on the Pinewood estate opposite the studio. Pinewood itself was fully utilized as it had been in *Sergeant*—where the studio entrance was the barracks entrance, for instance—and there are probably more corners of the studio on screen in the *Carry On* films than in anything else—even the studio publicity video!

Helping Hands

Windsor was featured again in the next outing, *Regardless,* about a group of odd-job people at the "Helping Hands" agency. The "shop front" was off a side road that was also used in *Loving* 20 years later. The regular cast members returned: Sid, Kenny W. Kenny C. Joan, Charlie and boy did we have fun. One of the guest stars in that film was the king of gobbledygook, Stanley Unwin. If you can tell me what he said was scripted, I wouldn't believe you! Then there was the delightful Esma Cannon. A tiny little creature but so full of fun. I do remember dear Kenny Williams getting landed with a job, in the story, of looking after

Kenneth Williams (and friends) are carrying on regardless for the Helping Hands agency in *Carry On Regardless.*

"I'll take you, but not your brother" was the response from the taxi driver (the bus conductor was a little more fruity) in *Carry On Regardless*.

a chimpanzee for the day—almost like you or I might a friend's dog. Anyway, they go off for a walk and on the way home—obviously feeling tired—Kenny's character decides to hail a cab. Up it pulls. "Where to guv?" The driver then sees the chimp and says," 'I'll take *you* but not your brother!" and drives off. Oh that's a lovely, funny scene. One of my favorites. It was harmless sort of humor. Later on, and I think people will agree here, the humor did degenerate somewhat towards the more saucy end of the spectrum. In fact, I became quite conscious of this descent and when it came around to the late 1960s and *Carry On Up the Khyber* came around, I thought that was it. I knew exactly what that one was supposed to suggest and I thought it was time to move on if this was the way they were going. I was terribly naive in the event as *Khyber* probably rates as the best in the series.

I digress, however. *Regardless* holds more fond memories for me than the earlier ones, I guess, because it was the film on which I was promoted from camera operator to director of photography. Ted Scaife had been d.p. with the company, but when this film came around he was offered

The finale of *Regardless* with the gang.

another (probably bigger) picture and so went off to do that. I meanwhile, stepped in and never looked back.

Life on the Ocean

There were big plans in store the following year. The next film was to make the leap from black-and-white to color with *Carry On Cruising* (1962). The big plans didn't, however, extend to big locations. The boat was all on a stage! The films were becoming quite popular and as a result I think the distributors felt a little more comfortable spending a few more pounds on color film stock. I think that particular entry also opened up the feel of the films, from small confined ones to quite lavish—"lavish" doesn't mean lots of money is needed, it's just how you show it on screen. The art director, a very talented chap named Alex Vetchinsky, did marvels on that film. The boat consisted of about 40 feet of port side, a few interiors of cabins, dining room, kitchens, etc. and part of the bridge. It was quite minimal but as I've always said, if the characters are

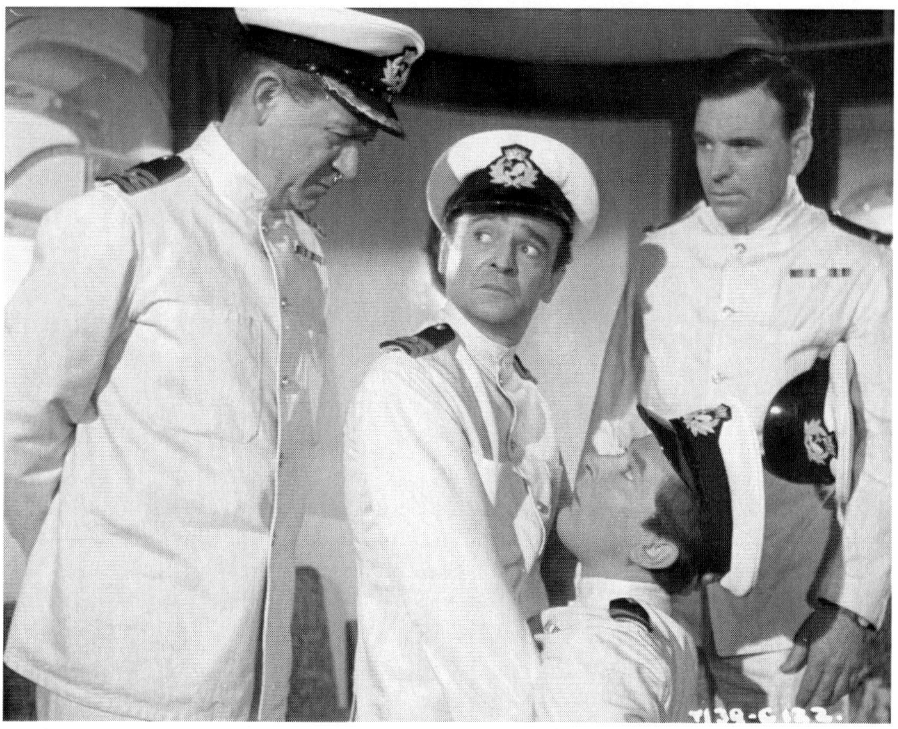

Sid James, Kenneth Connor and Kenneth Williams head up the crew in the all-at-sea comedy, *Carry On Cruising*.

good and the lines are good, people don't notice what's necessarily *not* there!

One of the most genial and charming films of the series was *Cabby*, which was very "Ealingesque" in style. That had a wonderful feel to it. It also saw us making extensive use of the surrounding roads of the studio. Sid's Cab Yard was actually (what is now) Car Park One at Pinewood, and I remember that particular set well because I used to drive to work in my first-ever car, a Morris 12. I also had a Lambretta which I often used, as I only lived up the road in Fulmer, to get in. This particular day both my car and the Lambretta were at the studio—I'd left the car the night before after going on for a drink and getting a lift home. There was a scene involving Charlie Hawtrey driving the taxi, Peg 1. Now, Charlie couldn't drive and so the crew taught him the basics, to appear convincing on film. In the process of doing so, he bashed into my car and then straight into the Lambretta. Talk about a whirling dervish. Thankfully, he didn't do much damage but it's ironic that of all the vehicles in the studio, and indeed used in that one film, he had to hit both of mine.

Peter Rogers would have gone mad had Charlie hit one of the black cabs of the "Glam Cabs" on site as they were all on loan to the production; it didn't so much matter with mine!

The film also marked the debut of a young actor called Jim Dale, who later went on to become a mainstay of the series throughout the 60s and then went on to greater things in America. I believe Gerry and Peter had spotted Jim in *Raising the Wind* in which he played a musician at the back of the orchestra. They were so pleased with his performance that they brought him back.

Eye-Spy

Jim Dale had a much bigger role in *Spying,* which was a great send-up of the Bond films, which at the time were riding high. I suppose it also "borrowed" bits from *The Third Man* with all those lovely scenes in Vienna ... which of course (I know that you're already thinking it,) was Pinewood's backlot. In came a young actress by the name of Barbara Windsor on that one too. Phwooor! I'll never forget that Vetch, the art director, was sitting in rushes watching the Viennese street scenes. He turned to me at the end and said, "Alan, that was very, very good, Very well lit." That was quite a compliment as Vetch was a man with a long list of wonderful and enviable credits. He'd worked with the greats, including Hitchcock. Mind, he was quite an eccentric and as well as being a terrible old scruff (often with toes peeping out of holes in his shoes) he'd be reading the script over breakfast and leave pieces of bacon in it to act as page markers. Rarely would you see him designing sets, it was all in his head and he'd make quick sketches on the back of a cigarette packet or something similar. He was very economical though—he had to be—and only did what was absolutely necessary; but it worked brilliantly.

It was all out at sea again in the next picture, *Jack,* set at the time of Nelson. There was quite an elaborate build on this one, with a ship constructed on the old backlot (now the 007 Stage) so we could get the real sky and clouds in shot and built it on a rostrum, to move it around as though bobbing on the sea. It was a bit tricky as far as I was concerned with the camera, as if I tried to get some height to look down on deck, I'd often see the car park in the corner of the frame! If memory serves, that was Juliet Mills' one and only *Carry On* film. There was some talk of casting Liz Fraser in the female lead, but she was unavailable or something like that, and in stepped Juliet. She'd worked with Gerry and Peter before in *Nurse On Wheels* so they all knew each other pretty well, and of course her dad (John) and sister (Hayley) were mainstays of Pinewood too. We had some laughs on that one, and I remember one scene when after the character played by Bernie Cribbins (who was back after his first appearance in *Spying*) had 50 lashes, Charlie Hawtrey tried to soothe his sore back with pepper ... as they'd run out of salt! Wonderful, wonderful fun. Sadly, the film wasn't as successful as the others had been. It didn't have the innuendo-filled gags, or cackling Sid James, so maybe that was partly the reason?

Infamy

Meanwhile, at Pinewood, there had been a big fuss over a film that had spent a fortune but hardly shot anything. It was, of course, *Cleopatra* with Elizabeth Taylor. It then set up again in Rome, and was still hitting the headlines—not necessarily for the reasons the producer may have wanted, though. It was only a matter of time therefore before Peter decided to mount a gentle send-up. Not that it was so gentle, mind, as they even ended up in court over their poster being too similar to the *Cleopatra* one. Anyway, around came *Cleo* and the most lavish entry in the series. I think it was immortalized in film history by Kenneth Williams' (as Caesar) line "Infamy! Infamy! They've all got it in for me!"

There was a myth going about that Peter Rogers had used the sets

Amanda Barrie, playing Cleopatra, takes a dip whilst the filmmakers take a few liberties with her story in *Carry On Cleo*.

abandoned by Twentieth Century–Fox. That's rubbish. We built our own and a wonderful art director named Bert Davey created some smashing sets. Cleopatra's bath, where Amanda Barrie sits in milk, for instance—that's a gem and looked every bit as good as the Fox sets did! A lot of effort went into making it all look good (including a square wheeled bike), and very highly polished. It paid dividends. Again, though, it was only a six-week shoot and no more than an absolute maximum of two cameras—it doesn't take any longer to shoot a film with more costumes and more lavish sets. Talbot Rothwell's script was marvelous too. He was such a brilliant writer, although later on the humor did rely a little too much on cruder innuendoe's for my liking.

I think some of the actors were hoping for a little more money once they'd seen the spectacle of the production, but that wasn't to be. Many later moaned a lot about how Peter and Gerald made a fortune from video and TV sales and they got nothing but their original flat fee. I think some of the main cast should have had a little tiny percentage. I say that mainly because I've just learned of a scheme in Germany whereby any of my

***Carry On* producer Peter Rogers feeds his director Gerald Thomas his breakfast.**

Top: On set with Gerald Thomas and Peter Rogers—showing he is a producer with a heart, with star Kenneth Williams. _Right:_ Discussing a set-up, Peter Rogers and Gerald Thomas on location in Windsor for one of the _Carry On_ films.

films (as director of photography) released on video there will result in my receiving a fee. It's tiny, and I should imagine only a few pounds, but if Germany can do it—and it relates to the lead artists, director, producer, musician, writer, art director and d.p.—I can't see why Britain couldn't do something like that. Mind you, I'm not sure how well the *Carry On* films did in Germany!

Get Off Your Horse…

For the next film, *Cowboy*, they did a marvelous job in transforming Pinewood's backlot into a Wild West town. That was a wonderful parody and one of the few films—if the only—in the series where American accents were adopted by the main cast. Nowadays, they'd just bring in American artists, but our guys showed they could act! Arizona, meanwhile, was doubled for by Camberley sand dunes where the army used to carry out tank maneuvers. My goodness, I even remember us having caterers on that one so it must have been a big location shoot and an hour from the studio.

As quite a few guns were used, the cast had a little instruction on safe use of them (they were only blank-firing though). There was also need for some actors to ride horses and use bow and arrows—the Red Indians mainly. Well, that was fun. On the Pinewood backlot, we had 200 people roll up for 50 available jobs. A horse-master was hired in "interview" the hopefuls. Most who claimed they could ride could hardly have got onto a bus without help, let alone a horse. So there was this scene of

The story of how the West was lost. Marshall P. Knutt (Jim Dale) braves outlaws and thugs, against the advice of Judge Burke (Kenneth Williams).

One of the British cinema release posters.

dozens of people riding up and down, arrows flying through the air, horses throwing riders … it was chaos!

Never one to miss a good spoof opportunity, Peter Rogers next thought about the Hammer Horror films which were doing great trade at the cinemas, and so in came *Carry On Screaming*.

Sid James wasn't around for that one, but they brought in Harry H. Corbett as a guest lead. He'd achieved great fame as Harold in *Steptoe and Son* on BBC TV, so was well-known to audiences. He was a charming chap, funny and always knew his lines. We had great fun with him and Fenella Fielding in the scenes where Harry swallowed the werewolf potion and transformed into the hairy beast—a little bit of genius in photography and editing there, if I may say so.

Around this time, Anglo-Amalgamated's Stuart Levy died. He loved the film and had backed them all. His partner Nat Cohen wasn't quite as enthusiastic and we knew things were going to change soon. They did, and not for the better. Peter Rogers didn't hang around though, and found a new backer for the series in Rank, parent company of the studio where he'd made the films.

Enter Rank

There was some concern over the *Carry On* prefix if memory serves, when Rank's Managing Director John Davis was fearful of Anglo suing him for "pinching" their title. It was all rubbish as Peter owned the title, but money people tend to get very worried at the thought of any litigation, and to save the series falling into legal limbo, it was agreed to proceed without the "Carry On" prefix. Hence resulted *Don't Lose Your Head* and *Follow That Camel.* Ironically, in later years they were both prefixed by the "Carry On" tag again.

The first was a wonderful take on the Scarlet Pimpernel and French Revolution; only here our hero was the Black Fingernail. Needless to say, Pinewood substituted for everywhere ... apart from the French chateau, which was doubled for by Waddesdon Manor near Aylesbury! For *Camel* we did venture out on location again. Blimey, two locations in the space of a few films. Well, it wasn't too far afield—Camber Sands in Sussex, to be truthful. That was our desert.

For the full effect, a camel was hired in. Her name was Sheena and she came from one of the far-flung, more exotic corners of Surrey. A zoo to be more accurate. I don't know if she had seen much in the way of sand, as out she came of her trailer (more of a horse box than star dressing room) and she point-blankly refused to walk on the sand. The road, yes, but sand, no. She didn't really know what this strange substance was. Never ones to be out maneuvered, we acquired some aircraft landing strips and placed them a few inches underneath the sand—it did the trick. Isn't it unbelievable?

There was a lovely scene with the camel and six or seven of the actors, including Kenny Williams, Jim Dale, Phil Silvers and Charles Hawtrey, and suddenly they all seemed to line up behind the camel—totally spontaneously—and we had this wonderful shot going over the sand dune. Had we planned it, it'd never have happened like that!

The weather wasn't brilliant up there. The day before we arrived, all of the potted palm trees had blown over and had to be replanted, and one day we had a touch of snow. Gerry said, "Put on a yellow filter and call it a sand storm." What can I say?

Carry On Doctor saw us back in a hospital for fun and frolics, but then I made a decision that I later regretted. Many people regard *Carry On Up the Khyber* as the pinnacle of the series. I agree, it is. In hindsight that is. You see, I was offered the film but turned it down for reasons I've already touched upon. I felt the series was becoming cruder and the great subtle comedy was lost in favor of saucier lines and glimpses of bums and tits. I knew full well what "Khyber Pass" is Cockney rhyming slang for and I said, "No thank you, not for me!" In stepped Ernest Steward and, boy, did they do a great job of sending up the British Raj in India during Queen Victoria's reign. The one I didn't do is the best!

Back Again

I did however, return a few films after, for *Carry On Henry,* another costume picture, this time set at the time of Henry VIII. Great use was made of royal locations around Windsor. The "Royal Drive" was used and Peter Rogers had gained permission for Sid James (who was playing Henry) and his entourage to ride down from Windsor Castle to Ascot across the Royal Park, down this famed grassland. Peter was very good at getting permission to film; even in those circles! I remember we used Maidenhead Town Hall in a few of the films, and you can imagine the to-ing and fro-ing of people around there, and civil servants attitudes as to the importance of their work. But it never caused a problem. We were pretty quick, and achieved everything with the minimum of disruption. It was also wickedly funny to be around a *Carry On* set and so people used to fall over backwards to help out.

I fancied a bit of sunshine and warm weather after *Henry* and so when Gerald asked me to work with him on *Carry On Abroad* I jumped at it. Perhaps I should have thought for a moment and asked exactly where "abroad" they had in mind ... it turned out that we didn't venture further than Pinewood's backlot. I should have guessed. It rained most of the time and was freezing bloody cold too!

The hotel set exterior on the lot was only about 20 foot high, the rest was added in later using matte techniques whereby an image "painted" onto the film is overlaid, giving the impression of a bigger building. Add in a bit of white gravel and sand and, presto, there is Spain.

The whole joke was that the hotel wasn't ready when the guests arrived and then it began falling apart. The final sequence was just that—the whole damn thing falling apart. That was fun!

For the next one, *Carry On Girls,* we ventured down to Brighton, which doubling for the fictional seaside town of Fircombe with the country's highest rainfall rate. To try and spice up tourism, a beauty contest was called.

It was a nice enough film and had most of the team of regulars to star, but to be honest, in comparison to some of the earlier films I'd been on, it seemed a bit lame. I think that the good ideas had been used and now the writer, Talbot Rothwell, was left with flimsier plots and cruder jokes. Certainly the last *Carry On* I made in the 1970s was the crudest (and worst) of the lot—*Emmannuell*e.

Risqué

At the time, the *Confessions* films were very popular and were regarded as soft porn to be honest. I think Peter and Gerald were feeling a bit of pressure from that series and decided to spice up the *Carry Ons* with a 15 certificate film. It backfired. The script was weak, in favor of nudity, and the increasingly risqué dialogue turned out to be a turn-off.

This was the last *Carry On* film as we know it. Sid James had already died, along with the lovely Hattie Jacques. The rest of the gang (Kenny Williams, Kenny Connor, Joan Sims, Peter Butterworth, Jack Douglas and the like) still lifted the film with their performances, but that magic spark seemed to have gone.

One Final Carry On

I went on to other things while Peter and Gerald kept busy with the TV compilations and plans for future films (which alas never materialized), and we kept in touch. You can imagine my delight when, 16 years later, the telephone rang and it was Gerald saying that they were going to do another *Carry On*. It was 1992 and the 500th anniversary of Columbus' voyage to the New World. Ridley Scott was making a big screen version, as was my old mate John Glen; but their versions were very serious pieces. I knew what ours would be—a great laugh! I did, to be honest, have another film—a rather big film—on offer, but because of the friendship which existed between Peter, Gerald and me, and because they had given me my break as a director of photography all those years ago, I couldn't *not* do *Carry On Columbus*. I'm really pleased I did actually, as it was dear Gerald's last film. A year or so later, he passed away.

The film wasn't the success we hoped. There were so few of the original team left—only Jim Dale, Jack Douglas, Bernard Cribbins, Jon Pertwee and a couple of others. In place of the others, in came the contemporary (television) comedians. It just didn't click. The script wasn't that funny—something Peter Rogers kept telling the producer John Goldstone. Peter served as executive producer on this one as it was really Goldstone who approached Gerry Thomas with the idea of a comedy spoof on Columbus, and then it eventually worked around to him saying "Let's do it as a *Carry On*." Peter, of course, owned the *Carry On* tag and so that's how he became involved.

I hoped it would be the most successful of the three Columbus movies (I think it actually was in the UK) but that little spark just wasn't there. Production values were high, though, and it was the most expen-

Top: Invasion of the Hume family—Alan, Simon Hume, actor Richard Wilson, and Martin Hume during *Carry On Columbus*. *Bottom:* Cast and Crew shot from *Carry On Columbus*.

sive film in the series. We had a lovely big set on E-Stage with the ship on it, and some painted background scenery—it looked pretty good. The ship didn't move so to give the impression of it casting off, we laid some track alongside it and moved the camera to the right. We stuck a chap (watching the ship going out) sitting on a bollard and we fixed it so as it was attached to the camera rig—as we moved, he moved, although on film he appeared to be stationary and the ship pulled forward to the left of the screen. Very clever!

It was only a year or so later that I heard Gerry Thomas had died. I was away on location and it hit me very hard. It was a Sunday lunchtime and all the family were sitting around for lunch, and he just collapsed and died. An awful shock for those around him, but a nice quick way to go.

I don't think there'll ever be another *Carry On* film. Peter says he hopes to put a TV series together, and there is talk of an animated series, *The Carryoons*, and certainly they remain popular through television and video ... and the fan base is massive! They're a lovely bunch and I often go along to gatherings with them.

Lots of things are talked about, but a lot of people ask me how much ad-libbing there was in the films, considering the bank of comedy talent involved. I can tell you, very little. Sure there were the odd one or two spontaneous lines or reactions that clicked, and Gerry would go for an extra take of it to make sure it really did work. In the main, however, the films were tightly scripted and scheduled and so left little room for much else—the story had to progress and unrelated jokes just weren't pertinent to driving the storyline.

There were great films to work on and a great gang of actors and crew involved. I remember them all very fondly.

V

From Operating to Lighting

After completing a couple of *Carry On* films, my next assignment was with Otto Heller and Egil Woxholt on *The Silent Enemy*. They were two amazing characters. Otto started out in his native Czechoslovakia and then moved to Germany where he photographed his first film in 1920, when he was around 24. From there he completed another 130 films before his death. A truly amazing record, and when you think his career encompassed films like *The Ladykillers, The Ipcress File, Alfie, Woman of Straw,* and *Peeping Tom,* it shows just how versatile and highly sought-after he was. Egil was a brilliant underwater photographer, and as much of this film was set underwater, he was drafted in. Egil went on to films like *Heroes of Telemark, Thunderball, On Her Majesty's Secret Service* and *Das Boot.* A formidable team, and there was little old me operating for them!

The story, shot in Gibraltar, was set on the Mediterranean in 1941 when the Italians started using underwater "midget submarines" to sink Allied ships. The Italians perfected this two-man motorized torpedo—not exactly a torpedo, but they sat on this thing with two seats and a battery-driven engine and with frogmen suits on. It became known as a chariot. They had a ship docked in Algaseras with underwater doors from which the submersible could be lowered into the ocean. They would then (already underwater) go across Gibraltar bay to Gib, cutting through the harbor defense nets, and place limpet mines on the side of ships. Initially, the British and Allies weren't aware of what was happening as they hadn't seen or tracked anything approaching the bay. It happened several times, with many ships sunk, and it seemed that neutral Spain was the base for activities. British Intelligence send out explosives expert Lionel Crabbe, but he finds only two British divers available to help him. It becomes a race against time, and it's a really exciting story—even more so because it was true. *The Silent Enemy* was a very apt title for the film.

Laurence Harvey, John Clements and Michael Craig played the leads and Sid James was in there too, (before he joined the *Carry On* cast regulars), as the petty officer in charge of physical training for the divers.

Laurence Harvey was a marvelous bloke, and quite a good swimmer. One day when we were at the hotel, next to a gigantic swimming pool, he said to me that he thought he could swim the entire length of this pool underwater. My colleagues and I were, shall we say, slightly doubtful and expressed as much in fruity language. Of course, he was then committed to doing it!

He put his cigarette out—he was always smoking—and took about ten deep breaths as he stood next to the side of the pool, and in he went. He swam about halfway underwater and slowly started to rise, but he kept going with his head under, and then we saw the back of his neck turning orange and from orange to red—but he wouldn't come up for air, and eventually made it! He did a few diving stunts himself in the film too, as the British divers would be transported in a fast boat across the harbor and then at various points throw themselves backwards into the water with all the scuba gear on. Laurence did all that very happily.

The behind-the-scenes folks were an interesting lot too. It was written and directed by William Fairchild, who also wrote *Passage Home, The Seekers* and *Malta Story,* whilst the executive producers were John and James Woolf (sons of C. M. Woolf, the famous producer). James died a few years later, but his brother went on to great things—*The African Queen, The Day of the Jackal* and TV's *Tales of the Unexpected.* It was quite an assignment.

From here, it was off to Switzerland. It was all hard work, I assure you!

Walt Disney had embarked upon a scaled-up production program in Europe and I was asked to join the crew of one of his films, *Third Man on the Mountain.* It was the third of several Disney films I'm proud to say I worked on, having cut my teeth as an operator with Peter Ellenshaw's matte work a few years earlier. Ken Annakin, a man mentioned many times in my ramblings, was the director with Harry Waxman and George Tairraz as the lighting directors. George was quite experienced at working at high altitudes and on mountains, and hence his involvement. Even though I'm biased, there is some spectacular photography in this film, and it really was an outstanding place of beauty to work in any event. A distinguished cast included James MacArthur, Michael Rennie, Janet Munro, James Donald and Herbert Lom; it was the story—set in 1865—of a Swiss dishwasher and his dream of conquering the local mountain. Good, traditional family fare as you'd expect from Disney.

Watcha Shipmates

A lighter storyline came with *Watch Your Stern* from the Gerald Thomas–Peter Rogers stable. The *Carry On* films were an immediate success, but outside of them Peter and Gerald made other films, and this was one of them. Granted, most were in the *Carry On* comedy mold, and probably could have had the prefix added—in fact, I think it was added for the video release of *Watch Your Stern* which, as you might have guessed, was an ocean-going comedy, though we saw little ocean. It featured the usual old suspects Kenneth Connor, Eric Barker, Leslie Phillips, Hattie Jacques, Spike Milligan, Eric Sykes and Sid James. *No Kidding*, their next film together, was slightly different from the out-and-out comedy of the *Carry Ons* though, as it was set in a holiday home for deprived rich children … a tug on the old heartstrings as well as comedy. It was written by the (then current) *Carry On* screenwriter Norman Hudis and starred Leslie Phillips, Geraldine McEwan, Julia Lockwood, Noel Purcell, Irene Handl and Joan Hickson. A great bunch, and I'd just been working with most of them on *Watch Your Stern* so it was like a continuation albeit on different sets and with different costumes!

This film has a bit of a soft spot in my heart, as on it Peter and Gerald asked if I would like to become the lighting-cameraman, what we nowadays call the director of photography. Their usual lighting cameraman had been offered a big film in Turkey, and went out there for a few months and so an opportunity presented itself. They didn't need to ask twice! In a way, it was a role I was aspiring to, as it was the next rung on the ladder. I had a solid grounding in camerawork, having worked my way through the ranks, and dear Peter and Gerald thought I was ready to have a go at lighting, and were keen to give me my break.

DoP

So what exactly is a lighting cameraman, or director of photography, you ask? A good question indeed, as I've been calling myself one for 40 years!

Well, on major feature films and filmed television series, the person responsible for the image reproduction is not, as such, the man behind the camera—i.e., the camera operator. It is the director of photography (DoP). He will work with his gaffer (chief electrician), who himself has a crew of three or four guys along with a truck load of lighting equipment, rigs and generator. The DoP uses these lamps, plus a range of color filters, to create the look called for by the script. Hopefully satisfying the director's expectations! One might call it painting with light; a rather grandiose term but one worth thinking about. For instance, visualize walking through the studio door and seeing a vast set which has been constructed by the art department. It is here that the DoP has to use his creative ability to achieve the look and feel required to make the set "look real"—i.e., not a set at all!

I have to admit that I always felt more comfortable working in a studio situation, because of the total control I had over the light. Shooting on location is quite another matter, as one is often faced with the wrong weather conditions and perhaps short days (in winter months) and variations in natural light as days change. Obviously, the crew cannot spend time (as a rule) waiting for the right weather conditions, and so the DoP has to use his truck load of lighting equipment and filters to maintain a constant look throughout the location shoot. Needless to say, it's sometimes pretty difficult, but then again I guess that's what my job is all about and the more you do it, the better you get!

Tarzan

Although we didn't venture far for location work on the *Carry Ons*, which is where we're up to in the story, I did on my next film *Tarzan the Magnificent*. It was directed by the wonderful Robert Day who had helmed some marvelous films in the U.K., including the wonderful Peter Sellers starrer *Two Way Stretch*. One of the supporting actors in that film was in this one too, Lionel Jeffries. Lionel was, and is, great fun. We worked together later on when we had both progressed "up the ladder" so to say. More on which will follow.

Gordon Scott had, by now, established himself in the role of Tarzan, having made five films (this would be his last as the character, though) and Bob Day brought a great supporting cast in: Jock Mahoney, John Carradine, Charles Tingwell and Earl Cameron.

We spent a warm few weeks in Kenya making what has become regarded as one of the best Tarzan films, and certainly Scott's best. It was well-directed, scripted (both thanks to Bob Day) and acted. Bob was such a "gentleman director"—totally professional, brilliant both with actors and technically. As he had progressed himself, through the ranks of clapper boy and director of photography, he was particularly kind to us camera personnel! I worked with Bob again later on *The Avengers* TV series. Bob punctuated his film career with TV work, both in the U.K.

and America, and along with *Danger Man* and the aforementioned *Avengers* he went on to direct episodes of *Kojak, Logan's Run* and *Dallas,* to name but a few.

Back to Comedy

Raising the Wind saw me return to the Peter Rogers–Gerald Thomas fold at Pinewood. Again, it was a film much in the mold of the *Carry On*s in all but name. Bruce Montgomery wrote it, and scholars amongst you will recognize the name as being responsible for the music in the early *Carry On* films. You'd be right. The film was therefore, not unsurprisingly, set in a music academy and focused on the comic misadventures of students. Leslie Phillips, Kenneth Williams, Sid James, James Robertson Justice and Liz Fraser were amongst the stars, along with a young chap named Jim Dale. I mentioned earlier that it was really through Jim appearing in this film that Gerry and Peter "noticed" him and took him under their wing, making him a star of the *Carry On* films.

The story goes that Jim, a pop singer at the time with a few hits under his belt, had an audition for a role of a second trombone player in an orchestra (which was conducted by Kenneth Williams). There were just a few lines and Kenny had to say, "Where's your music?" to which Jim replied "Oh, I haven't got it … oh, yes I have … I was sitting on it all the time." And he then produced his music, a bit crumpled and so on. Jim had obviously decided that his "big chance" wouldn't really create much of an impression, with just a line or two, so he decided to make fun of Kenny Williams. When Kenny said in his typical nasal, fruity voice, "Where's your music," Jim delivered his line in exactly the same voice. He was a terrific mimic of Kenny. We all fell about laughing.

Kenny meanwhile walked very quickly over to Gerry Thomas and began scowling and pointing at Jim. I thought, "Oh, no, that's it. Jim has upset Kenny so he'll be out."

In fact, what Kenny said was, "You ought to really use this young man more. Anyone who has that much cheek ought to be in the *Carry On* films." And, when we started the next *Carry On*, Jim was there!

I remember another funny little incident on that shoot. We were on location somewhere, quite a suburban area in London, and there was myself, the first assistant, the director, the producer, and the art director. It was pouring with rain and very gray, and we were all huddled in a little group talking about what we'd do. We were there some time when I spotted this little old lady shuffling along towards us. She shoved right into the middle of the group and produced a flyer, handing it to me. On it was written "And God said, *Let there be light.*" It so amused me, as she could have given it to any one of us, but chose me the lighting director. I quietly handed it to the director, he chuckled and gave it to the producer whilst the lady shuffled off down the road!

In the Doghouse was next, and I again found myself working with some of the good folks in front of the camera from my previous film. It was a comedy (of errors) following the adventures of a newly qualified vet, Leslie Phillips. Darcy Conyers directed. He actually started out as an actor, progressed quickly to producer and then director. A likable chap, born in Tanzania, he didn't make another film after this and died very young in 1973 at the age of 54. The producer was a wonderful fellow named Hugh Stewart. Hugh was a name we all knew around Pinewood. He started out in the cutting rooms at Denham and edited films for such prestigious directors as Alfred Hitchcock, Michael Powell and Victor Saville. He'd been a fixture at Pinewood since the War years actually, with the Army Film and Photography Units out on the front lines producing some very important documentaries, including *Tunisian Victory*. After the War he produced his first feature, *Trottie True* (in which my mate Roger Moore had an early "extra" role). Hugh was very much a gentleman of the business and a very creative producer who got on well with the great Sir Alexander Korda, who was by then with MGM. Hugh fell ill before, *Bonnie Prince Charlie,* on which he was due to work, and during his recuperation read *Trottie True*. He wanted to film it. MGM weren't keen and so he took it to Two Cities, which was controlled by Rank. Hugh stayed with Rank for nearly 20 years and went on to produce ten Norman Wisdom comedies and two films with Morecambe & Wise.

Daffodils

Twice Round the Daffodils was the big screen version of a successful play called *Ring for Catty* which had been written by actor Patrick Cargill and Jack Beale. I know Peter Rogers had wanted to make the film for a few years, and after the success of *Sergeant*, suggested it for his next subject. Nat Cohen of Anglo-Amalgamated (Peter's backers) turned it down flat (again!). It was a rather somber comedy set in a sanatorium for patients suffering from tuberculosis. Cohen wanted another *Carry On*. Peter asked his screenwriter Norman Hudis to take the play and use it as a source for a "hospital"-set *Carry On*. The film that followed, with great success, was *Nurse*. But there was relatively little of the original story left in this screen version.

Never one to miss an opportunity, Peter realized that the *Catty* script was barely used. Hudis was brought in to script *Twice Round the Daffodils,* which was a much more faithful adaptation of the play. It also ensured Patrick Cargill received two royalty checks—one for *Nurse* and the other for *Daffodils,* as both were based on his play. What a position to be in!

I certainly wouldn't describe *Daffodils* as a film in the *Carry On* vein. It was a much more serious subject, though one in which Peter saw the black humor which arose from patients finding themselves in hospital for a relatively long period, away from loved ones. Anglo-Amalgamated remained unsure, but they wanted more *Carry On*s, which had made them a fortune to date, and bowed to Peter's judgment.

Many familiar faces were included in the cast: Kenneth Williams, Joan Sims, Juliet Mills, Donald Sinden and Donald Houston, to name but a few. With Gerry Thomas at the helm, it proved great fun to work on. Around this time, Kenny Williams was also appearing on stage in the West End, and so was pretty tired during the day, especially under the hot studio lights. We often found him asleep in his hospital bed, in fact!

The title, by the way, referred to a flower bed in Pinewood's gardens—as usual with Peter and Gerry the film was shot all around Pinewood—and it was said that if the TB patients were fit enough to walk out into the garden, and walk around this large flower bed, full of daffodils—twice—then they were fit enough to be discharged.

The Iron Maiden **experiencing a few problems.**

Top: Michael Craig and Anne Helm. *Bottom:* The film's release poster.

Still Laughing

There was just no getting away from Gerry and Peter for me, but I wasn't complaining. Next on their production schedule was a charming, gentle comedy called *The Iron Maiden.* You may recall a very successful film called *Genevieve* which was made by Rank a few years prior to this, all about the London-to-Brighton Vintage Car Race. It was a massive success. I don't think Peter consciously tried to copy *Genevieve,* that wasn't his style, but he did see the potential in that "sort" of subject. He brought in Vivien Cox, who had been a friend since their days working for Sydney Box at Gainsborough, to co-write the screenplay with Leslie Bricusse.

Just as *Genevieve* hadn't strayed far from the Pinewood locale, neither did we with *The Iron Maiden*—a stretch of location between Beaconsfield and Amersham, which is about six miles from the studio in all! We shot mainly across country, but we had to shoot on the main road too, which involved a lot of stopping traffic for this old, slow engine to chug along. It was also a film of a period a few years earlier, and so we had to be careful not to get modern cars in shot on the road! The vehicle at the center of the film, and indeed the title, was a large traction engine, driven by actor Michael Craig, who was playing an aircraft designer with a greater passion for traction engines than aircraft. Cecil Parker, Alan Hale, Jr., and Lionel Jeffries co-starred. It was, like always, great fun and a charming film but it didn't manage to recreate the success of *Genevieve* or even the *Carry On*s for that matter. Perhaps the charm of classic, vintage cars was more identifiable than a great traction engine?

Undeterred, Peter and Gerry moved on to preparing their next project with another medical theme. Before I get to that, though, I meanwhile joined my old friend Sidney Hayers, who had been an excellent editor before turning his hand to directing, on a film called *This Is My Street.* We later worked together again, most memorably, on *The Avengers* and *Space Precinct,* and a few movies between too. I'd been working in color on the recent Peter Rogers films, but this went back to black-and-white which, I thought, helped the film as it was a particularly grotty, "kitchen sink" type story. Call me an old romantic if you like, but that really came across in the shadowy, moody black-and-white photography far better than it would have in color. Bill MacIlwraith adapted Nan Maynard's novel of a Battersea housewife having an affair with her mother's lodger, and June Ritchie, Ian Hendry with a young John Hurt starred.

During one day's scheduling on the film, we traveled to Southend in Essex to film numerous shots at the funfair before driving all the way back to complete some evening shots near Hammersmith fly-over, in a flat, and then journeyed back to Pinewood to film a few night shots. That was quite a day, but it had to be done and done it was. Some people say how the unions were all-powerful back then and there were strict rules about finish times and what have you. Yes, that was the case, but if you had a good crew, a good assistant director and so on, invariably if we needed to do a bit extra, we did. We never lost sight—or at least *I* never did—of the fact the film was the priority.

Nurse On Wheels was next and a *Carry On* in all but prefix. Peter and Gerry's forays into the medical world had proven successful to date, but this was slightly different in that it wasn't set in a hospital, but in the country—following a district nurse on her travels. Norman Hudis came back to write the script, and we went back to using black-and-white, for budget reasons I guess. In came Juliet Mills, John's daughter, as the titular mobile nurse; other stars included Ronald Lewis and Joan Sims. Joan was such wonderful fun, so bubbly and so funny. She played a Welsh girl in this film and, to my mind, stole the show. It's so sad that she died in 2001, so suddenly. If memory serves, Joan was originally cast in the lead role, of Joanna Jones, but unfortunately her weight problem, which became more of a problem in later life, meant the romantic scenes might appear a little unconvincing and after much discussion it was decided to re-cast. Joan did, though, still get paid the same fee as agreed previously.

A Bit of Horror

What was next? *The Kiss of the Vampire.* Oh yes, I liked that one. That was a Hammer production over at the famous Bray Studios. Anthony Hinds produced, and Don Sharp directed.

For *me* the interesting thing with this film was that I could play around a bit with my lighting to create an eerie, moody atmosphere. Unlike many other "Hammer Horrors," this film relied less on blood and gore to scare its audience, and more on atmosphere. It was quite chilling, in fact. Gerald and Marianne Harcourt's car breaks down and they have to spend a few days in a small, remote village whilst it is repaired. It doesn't take long before they are invited to the castle of Dr. Ravna, he being the leader of a vampire cult. Clifford Evans, Edward de Souza, Noel Willman and Jennifer Daniel starred.

Bray was and is a lovely studio. It was originally built around the old house, Down Place, a seventeenth century mansion once owned by bookseller Jacob Tonson. He formed the "Kit Kat Club" there with the Earl of Dorset as Head. All members were distinguished for their rank, learning and wit; many holding important government positions. It remained a private residence until 1949 when it was sold and it became Bray Studios and synonymous with Hammer. Of course Hammer was around earlier, and was making films (not least at Beaconsfield), but under James Carreras the new Hammer was now born, and based at Bray.

Horror films didn't really feature in Hammer's early output. In fact, it wasn't until the mid–1950s when Carreras secured the film rights to the TV series *The Quatermass Experiment*, and the phenomenal success it enjoyed, that horror became a genre in the Hammer portfolio. In 1956 *The Curse of Frankenstein* went before the cameras and made stars of Peter Cushing and Christopher Lee; whilst firmly establishing the "Hammer House Of Horror."

They went on to produce up to eight films a year and developed a massive cult following. In 1968, the company received the Queen's Award for Industry in recognition of its overseas earnings, and the next year James Carreras was knighted.

The 1960s saw the whole industry struggle and Hammer did not escape. The company gave up their Bray Studios and moved to other facilities to continue their production program. Bray continued to operate under a number of new owners, and continues to operate as a fully functioning film and television studio to this day. It stands on the River Thames and is very intimate with just a few stages, compared to the 20 or so stages each at studios like Pinewood and Shepperton, but maintains a wonderful atmosphere and reputation. Down Place is now a luxury hotel.

VI

Enter Amicus and John Steed

In a similar vein, if you'll forgive the pun, came my next film *Dr Terror's House of Horrors*. It wasn't from the Hammer fold but Amicus, and produced by Milton Subotsky, who also wrote the script. Now there's a fascinating character, and one whom I worked with again later in life. He was born in New York in 1921 and made his first film 36 years later—it was a musical of sorts called *Rock, Rock, Rock*. That led to another similar film before he took a totally different direction with *The City of the Dead*. From there he wrote and / or produced almost 40 more films. It was in the horror genre I suppose he enjoyed most success; not gruesome horror as we see nowadays, horror that leaves nothing to the imagination, but more—dare I say—intellectual horror.

This film was really the first "compendium" of horror tales from Milton. He followed it up with *Tales from the Crypt, From Beyond the Grave, Vault of Horror* and *Asylum*. There was a damn good cast in Peter Cushing, Ursula Howells, Roy Castle, Christopher Lee and Donald Sutherland. I liked them all—immensely. I later worked with Peter and Christopher again, as I did Donald. Without wanting to alienate the others, Donald Sutherland is one of my favorite actors. More of him later.

We were based, if memory serves me correctly, out of Shepperton Studios with a pretty tight budget and my old friend Freddie Francis directing. Freddie had, of course, been a director of photography himself (and he's won two Oscars along the way!) and was now turning his hand to direction. It was a genre he more or less stuck with in his directorial assignments. I suppose it's the old typecasting again; he had some success with horror films, and that's what he was offered. Freddie was a marvelous guy to work for, and he never once told me what to do. Yes, we discussed ideas and thoughts, but he did not "light" the film nor try to.

The "top and tale" of the stories were in a railway carriage, as the film followed five characters in the carriage, who are told—by virtue of a mysterious sixth passenger's tarot cards—about their own grisly demise. Peter was, of course, the sixth passenger, the titular Dr Terror who, in a way, linked it all together. His character was in fact called Dr Schreck but I guess that didn't quite work as a title!

Far removed from his often-evil characterizations, Peter Cushing was the gentlest of the gentle. He kept himself pretty much to himself, there was no air of grandeur about him, and he always knew his lines. A dream. I'd first worked with him on *The End of the Affair* in 1954 when I was operating for Wilkie Cooper. That was more of a romantic role than anything else he is (now) remembered for; it was Hammer that changed it all later in the decade. Van Johnson and Deborah Kerr were the stars of that film, and I remember one day Johnson saying to Wilkie Cooper, "Make me look old—give my face some character." Van's face had that in following years.

Headwear

Three Hats for Lisa was Sid Hayers' next film, on which he asked for me to join him. Leslie Bricusse and Talbot Rothwell (of *Carry On* fame) wrote this musical which still looks good, if I may say so. I suppose it was a small-scale film, with a small story, but it attracted Sid James, Sophie Hardy, Una Stubbs, Peter Bowles and Joe Brown. It was all about how a docker and a taxi driver offered to help a foreign actress (French I think) to steal three typically English hats. We worked mainly on location around London and it was a pretty short schedule. Jack Hanbury was the producer but, somewhere down the chain, there was Peter Rogers. I know Peter had a lot of influence on these small films whether it be through finance, his distribution interests or through his contracted personnel—such as his writers and me!

It wasn't surprising therefore that Peter should be at the helm of the next film I worked on. It was with him as producer, and Gerry Thomas as director. It was, I guess, a Carry On in all but name; it was called *The Big Job*. All the "usual suspects" were back, including Sid James, and the story involved a daring and, naturally, big bank robbery. In fact, a lot was filmed in my local village of Chalfont St Giles. The bank exterior in the village is actually a pub in real life (and coincidentally it also featured as a bank in the big screen version of the BBC comedy *Dad's Army*).

Had we had the time to indulge in liquid refreshment, it would have been quite handy, but I've already told you what our schedules were like on these films, so there wasn't much opportunity to loiter on "location."

Although I describe the films with Peter and Gerry as being modest budget and tightly scheduled, that isn't to say I thought any less of them. They were terrific guys to work with, great fun and it really wasn't like a job of work. I'd have done it for free. I shouldn't have said that!

Cliff

I also worked with Sid on another film that year with a young talented, up-and-coming pop singer named Cliff Richard. It was an easygoing comedy called *Finders Keepers* and all about how a young pop group (Cliff and his backing group The Shadows) find an American atomic bomb off the coast of Spain.

Dame Diana Rigg as Steed's most famous side-kick, Mrs. Emma Peel.

Cliff had made a few films before this, including the very successful *Summer Holiday*. Although this was pleasant enough, it didn't really take off in a big way, and I don't think there were any hit records that came out of it either. Shame, really.

I found Cliff and the others to be totally unspoiled and without pretension. He's remained one of the nice guys in show biz and a tireless charity worker for which he received a knighthood a few years back.

Steed & Co.

I shall progress on to my first TV series now I think, as it was a quite important addition to my résumé. *The Avengers.* I'm sure you will have all seen at least one episode of the show in your time, and as it still plays on TV around the world today, that's not an unreasonable assumption for me to make. The early episodes—and bonus points for those of you who remember Ian Hendry and then Honor Blackman as Steed's partners—were "live" every week. That had its problems and restrictions, but when the show was filmed for transmission at a later date, and location filming introduced, the show was given a new lease of life and, in my humble opinion, entered its golden period.

The show came together thus: Each episode would take ten days to film and ten days to complete (editing, dubbing, etc.) There would usually be two directors and two crews on the show, so as when one episode completed filming, that director was allowed time to supervise his post-production and prepare for the next; meanwhile, director number two and crew two would shoot another episode, with director two then going off to supervise his post-production ... and so the cycle continued. I worked on the show over three separate series. The first series, for me, lasted about 16 weeks. I went off and did a few other things, and then came back to complete some more episodes in the next series. I was, at this time you must remember, under contract to Peter Rogers, and he rented me out to the production. I think he did rather well out of it ... and he kindly gave me a "bonus" at the end of it.

My episodes were with Diana Rigg as Mrs Peel. Honor Blackman, who played Cathy Gale in earlier episodes, had left to go on to other things (in particular, the role of Pussy Galore in *Goldfinger*). Diana, who was already an accomplished actress, was quite honestly brilliant. She made the role her own and, with due love and respect to those before and after her in the series, made Mrs Peel the definitive side kick to Patrick Macnee's John Steed.

Diana was, and is still, very pretty although she had a squarish jaw, and her cheeks sank in a bit; but I made a particular effort to ensure she looked her most gorgeous on screen. It's my old adage—always make your leading ladies look good. I guess the front office must have been pleased with what I'd done because they kept me on. A few others came and went!

Pat MacNee is a super bloke, and a terrific guy to work with. I suppose he's been typecast as the suave leading man, a little like Roger Moore and Robert Vaughan have been, and he really does epitomize the English gentleman. He knew the character of John Wickham Gascone Berresford Steed pretty well. He's a fascinating guy actually, and started off his career as an uncredited extra in George Bernard Shaw's *Pygmalion.* He's appeared in shows as diverse as *Battle of the River Plate*, *Columbo*, *Battlestar Galcatica*, *The Sea Wolves*, *Sherlock Holmes* (many!) and one of my

Bond films, *A View to a Kill.* It was rumored that Pat was actually David Niven's cousin, but this was later found to be untrue and actually a little story his (rather eccentric) mother had made up—perhaps in the hope of furthering her son's career?

Update

Pat was the one constant in *The Avengers* throughout its run in the 1960s, and then later in the 1970s when they revived the show as *The New Avengers* with Gareth Hunt and Joanna Lumley. I never worked on that series, but did enjoy it. Sadly, it was a bit of a pickle financially, as there was French and Canadian money involved and they took the characters out of their natural South of England home and transposed them into foreign locales. It didn't quite work.

As for the 1990s feature film, I think we'll skip that.

Bob Asher, as mentioned, was one of the directors on the series; but in checking a few details on the show I was amazed to see that none fewer than 38 directors worked on the show between 1961 and 1969. I can't mention them all, but a few jump off the page: Roy Ward Baker, Peter Sykes, Ray Austin, Don Chaffey, John Hough, Leslie Norman ... They were all top-caliber directors, many coming from a film background. For me to rub shoulders with a lot of them, let alone work with them, was an honor.

Although schedules were tight, we always seemed to manage to have fun without feeling the endless pressures of delivering on time and budget. That always happened, though. It's just one of the ways the business has changed nowadays and become much more "serious." Much like the *Carry On* films, we didn't venture far from the studio for location work. In fact, I think "Avengerland" all falls within a few miles radius of Borehamwood. We did, of course, feature the cars quite a lot: Steed's Bentley and Mrs. Peel's Lotus. Those sequences were really responsible for opening up the show in terms of location work. We did some pretty hazardous stuff with them, to be honest, such as hanging off the side of the Bentley with a hand-held camera. It probably wouldn't happen nowadays either, with insurance and health and safety regulations. Another way in which the business has changed (probably for the better, I must add).

It's sad to see that of the half-dozen studios in Borehamwood, only a couple have survived. The BBC now run the one in Clarendon Road, and across the way Elstree Film Studios, where *The Avengers* was filmed, survives—although a fraction of its former size.

Patrick Macnee, as John Steed in *The Avengers*.

North of Watford

After *The Avengers,* I moved across to Watford and a tiny little studio in Bushey. It had quite a history actually, as it opened in 1913 when a wealthy father-and-son team, Sir Hubert and Siegfried von Herkomer, built a studio in the garden of their house, converted from an old chapel. A few films were made before, two years later, Herkomer died and the studio was taken over by the British Actors Film Company, which had A. E. (Matty) Matthews as chairman. They made a few films, notably with A. E. Matthews and Nelson Keys, often giving up salaries for a share of profits. In 1922, after having merged with the Alliance Company a couple of years earlier, the operation was wound up. Long periods of closure followed, though a couple of comedy films were made in 1924 and the following year Michael Balcon produced a number of Gainsborough burlesques there. The "Quota Quickies" saw a nice lease of life for the studio in the '30s under the ownership of Randal Terraneau. During the War, the buildings were used to store nitrate films, but then in the years after, Ambassador Film Productions took over and actors such as Michael Medwin, Sid James, Max Bygraves and Barbara Mullens made films there. Later it was used by the Children's Film Foundation, and later still for training and publicity films. In the late '70s and early '80s Michael Winner used it as a base. In 1985, the studios were closed and all but demolished.

We were there to make *The Bofors Gun*. That was a tough film. We shot mainly at night over a six-week schedule and it was freezing cold most of the time! The film was set in 1954, in Germany, when a British army unit (guarding the titular Bofors gun) runs into trouble when a violent and unstable Irish private (Nicol Williamson) picks on a weakly National Service corporal (John Thaw). Jack Gold directed a script by John McGrath (which was based on his play). It was really an expansion of what was a TV film, but there was truly excellent acting and one of the supporting actors, Ian Holm, won a BAFTA award.

Family Matters

Father, Dear Father was a popular TV series in the early 1970s and, like many others, received the big screen treatment. The film, of the same name, starred the same lead cast of Patrick Cargill (as Father) and Noel Dyson (as Nanny), with Richard O'Sullivan, Ursula Howells, Natasha Pyne ... and Donald Sinden. William G. Stewart directed (as he did the TV series, and indeed the TV series of *Bless This House*). There isn't a great deal to tell, apart from perhaps the fact that I was working with a TV director on one of his first films. That proved interesting. William was inclined to want to shoot everything all at the same time, and so we might have three of four cameras running. For instance, in a dining room scene I would normally—on a *Carry On*, say—have one camera and we'd do a long shot, mid-shot and then perhaps close-ups and over-the-shoulders shots, reaction shots and one by one the whole thing would come together. William wanted to capture it all together. So if Patrick Cargill's character said something funny, he'd want the immediate reaction from Noel Dyson as though it was happening live. Whereas what I would expect to do is the close-up on Patrick, then we'd stop move the camera and get the reaction shot from Noel all with one camera. It meant the actors had to repeat themselves in different takes, but that's screen acting technique. It may perhaps speed things up slightly, to have several cameras on such a scene, but you then weigh it up against the expense. Okay for big action scenes that are expensive and where you have to capture every inch of what's going on, yes, we'd get four or more cameras going, but on a small-scale interior I normally wouldn't. And remember, the more cameras you have shooting simultaneously, the more lights you need and the less space you have—and the less the ability to move the camera, as more often than not you'd have a certain movement (30 degrees say) and then another camera would be in frame. Anyway, it wasn't a problem but it did prove an interesting project to me, working this way.

The Big Heist

My next project happily involved Patrick Macnee again: *Mister Jericho,* a TV film directed by Sid Hayers and produced by Julian Wintle. It was a 'heist' story which we made out in Malta. It had quite an international cast, Patrick as already mentioned, Herbert Lom, Connie Stevens, Marty Allen, Leonardo Picroni, and Paul Darrow, with music by legendary Beatles producer George Martin and a wonderful song by Don Black. They were just making their mark in the film world! A couple of funny little stories spring to mind on this film. We were filming some speedboat sequences down there, on the ocean, and the "crooks" in our story were in these boats trying to escape the authorities. Our camera boat was following close behind to capture everything on celluloid. I guess we were moving at about 30 knots, which is quite fast, and the boats were creating quite substantial bow waves in their wake. We, of course, were riding on these waves from the getaway boat. So we have the camera operator on his hands and knees at the front of the boat, holding the camera, with Sid Hayers on his left holding him whilst I was on his right, holding him. After about a mile or so, Sid said to the driver, "Veer left and go across the wake." This he readily did. However, the boat flew up in the air and turned over. Sid Hayers disappeared out into the ocean, as did the operator, but I was still in there, fortunately along with the camera. Looking back a few hundred yards, we could see two heads bobbing up and down in the water! We went back to pull up Sid, who was covered in blood and minus his glasses and wristwatch and the operator was none too clever either. But Sid instigated that little bit of maneuvering, and boy, did he regret it.

From sea to land. Another chase sequence involved a Jeep speeding round the narrow roads of Malta, down the mountains and round the tight bends. Part way down, we met a lorry coming up the hill! The brakes went on, and Isaac Newton's laws prevailed—everything went flying forwards out of the camera car, including Sid Hayers who rolled down the road ... covered in blood again! Dear old Sid did bring so much on himself. You couldn't help but love him though.

Malta turned into familiar ground to me over the years, as I made about seven films on the gigantic water tank there. It's the largest in Europe and because it sits right on the edge of the ocean, it offers wonderful natural horizons out to sea. Well, there are two tanks actually on the southeastern side of the island. Mediterranean Film Studios (MFS), as it's called, boasts one indoor tank and two large exterior water tanks. In size the tanks are only second to Fox Studios' water facility in Baja, Mexico. However, the Malta tanks are far more inexpensive in my experience! It was formerly called Malta Film Facilities and hosted a large number of productions. Recent popular productions, I'm told, include Dino de Laurentiis' *U-571* (1999) and Ridley Scott's *White Squall* (1996). A considerable amount of TV commercials are also shot in the tanks each year.

But how did this former British colony, just 16 miles long, with a population of about 400,000, come to attract such a disproportionately large quota of major projects you ask? Good question.

The Malta Tank

In 1963, a British special-effects specialist, Jim Hole, was working on a Viking saga, *The Long Ships*, when a storm off the Spanish coast destroyed the production's floating sets and models. Surveying the debris, Jim decided there must be safer, more controlled, ways to film on water and created the perfect alternative at Rinella, on Malta's eastern coast. There he and a young Maltese construction manager, Paul Avellino, built a shallow water tank 300 feet wide. The tank blends seamlessly with a clear horizon, so directors could give audiences the illusion of seaborne action taking place miles off the coast without relying on back projection.

The newly opened Malta Film Facilities welcomed its first client, the Cold War drama *The Bedford Incident*, in 1964, and movies with wet, if not always watertight, plots began flowing steadily towards Malta. *Murphy's War, Orca: Killer Whale, Raise the Titanic* (for which Lew Grade spent $1 million building a second and much deeper shooting tank and claimed it would have been cheaper in the end to have "lowered the Atlantic"), *Cutthroat Island* and *Swept Away* to name a few. Producers initially drawn to Malta for the tanks quickly recognized its other assets (as did I): a superb climate, easy access from major European cities and English-speaking craftsmen available at competitive rates. Above all, the cliffs, coastal inlets and medieval architecture of Malta and its twin island, Gozo, offer unspoiled locations that are a major draw for period dramas such as the $38 million *Count of Monte Cristo*.

See, you're learning!

Staying with water for a minute or two, my next production was *Captain Nemo and the Underwater City*. That was a fun picture, and a terrific cast: Robert Ryan, Chuck Connors, Bill Fraser, Kenneth Connor, and Nanette Newman. At the helm directing was James Hill, who I'd first worked with on *The Avengers*. Terrific guy.

The sets were designed by Bill Andrews. One of the very best underwater camera specialists, Norwegian Egil Woxholt, really helped show them off to the max. Sad to say, he is no longer with us.

It was filmed at the old MGM Studios in Borehamwood. They had a water tank on the lot, nowhere near as big as Malta nor even the one at the EMI Studios down the road where they filmed *Moby Dick*, but I'm pretty certain we did most of the water stuff on the tank at MGM. Probably one of the last productions in there. They were truly wonderful studios, I'd say by far the best in the country. They opened the doors there in 1948 and the keyword was glamour. It was typical of a powerful American film company. Big American stars came across: Spencer Tracy, Deborah Kerr, Robert Taylor, Elizabeth Taylor, Stewart Granger, Ava Gardner, Clark Gable and so on. They had a terrific backlot there too, and I recall they built a massive Chinese set there for *The Inn of the Sixth Happiness* in 1958. Sadly, in the '60s, the business was feeling the pinch of dwindling revenues (partly due to TV) and 1969 was known as the "year of the long knives" at MGM. Executives left in fast succession and the production program was minimal. In 1970, after disappointing box office on some of its films, MGM announced it was reducing losses within the company by closing the seven-stage British facility. The industry couldn't believe it. MGM immediately did a deal to use the EMI Studios down the road in Borehamwood, but meanwhile this terrific studio they'd opened a couple of decades earlier was left to decline and was eventually taken over by a cold storage company.

I guess I was lucky to have worked there, and indeed to be on one of the last films to be housed within the complex. Nowadays if you drive down from the A1 towards Borehamwood, you can't even guess there was once a great film studio on the site, let alone get a feeling for the great films produced there. Though the surrounding residential roads are ironically named after our film greats: (Will) Hay, (Margaret) Rutherford, (Vivien) Leigh, (Anthony) Hancock, (British) Lion, Gainsborough (Pictures) and so on. I wonder if the residents really know the history behind where they live?

Whilst it was now a quieter time in the business than a few years earlier, we were still doing pretty well for ourselves and keeping busy … well, *I* was, at least!

That Friday Feeling

Perfect Friday was my next picture, and a very enjoyable one too, directed by Peter Hall, now Sir Peter Hall. He had, of course, become famous as a theater director and this, I think, was his fourth film as director. It was a top-notch catch he'd assembled, headed by Ursula Andress, Stanley Baker and David Warner. It is the story of an excellent, intricate bank heist involving three uneasy partners (Baker, Andress and Warner) who plot a raid on the vaults of Baker's firm and steal £200,000. The plan is aborted on several tries amidst great tension, until the elements finally fall into place on a "perfect Friday." There is also some added suspense of who will double-cross who, along with a great finale.

It was a big film for me, and I think for Peter Hall. He was a very charming man and knew what he wanted from his artists. He wasn't a screamer and shouter and he listened intently to his crew, in particular me, when it came to technical aspects and ideas. After all, theater and cinema are two very different worlds—and he knew that, so it made our relationship a particularly happy one.

The music was interesting too, as they brought in Johnny Dank-

Stanley Baker leads the cast on *The Last Grenade*.

Honor Blackman and Richard Attenborough lend solid support as father and daughter in *The Last Grenade.*

worth, who'd worked on quite a lot of films and on *The Avengers*. He, of course, is famous for working with Cleo Laine too.

War

The Last Grenade was a very important and dramatic film for me, directed by Gordon Flemyng. It was based on John Sherlock's *The Ordeal of Major Grimsby*, quite a violent war-based melodrama with Stanley Baker, Alex Cord, Honor Blackman, Richard Attenborough, Julian Glover, John Thaw and Ray Brooks. A Congo-set film too, in which we moved to Hong Kong as Stanley's character (Grimsby) pursued a double-crosser. It was a tight shoot, and pretty tough weather too, as I'm sure you can imagine. (We shot all of it in Spain so it wasn't quite Congo weather, but hot enough.) I recall that Stanley Baker, with the greatest of respect, wasn't very good at taking direction. He was quite a heavyweight actor by then, and producer too, so thought he knew better than the director, and better than me when it came to lighting techniques. He listened, but used to like to then do things his way. I think it caused swords to be crossed a few times with Gordon, but obviously they were both professionals and we eventually got on with the job in hand. I suppose that happens with actors, maybe more so nowadays, because they're built up to great heights and as such feel that they know, or should know, better than everyone else. Some get a bit touchy about how they're lit, and only want certain profiles. It can be tedious, but then again, I want to make them look good, so it's in my best interest to try and be helpful, and sometimes bite my tongue!

Shirley MacLaine

Another terrific Hollywood leading lady is Shirley MacLaine. Of course, she was famous for her many film appearances from her early films such as *The Trouble With Harry* (1955), *Around The World In Eighty Days* (1956) and then *The Apartment* (1960), *Gambit* (1966) and *Two Mules for Sister Sarah* (1969). However, this project—*Shirley's World*—was a 17-part, 30-minute TV series produced by the late, great Lew Grade. Ray Austin, who used to be a stunt man actually, wrote and directed. He'd directed a lot of other shows for Lew such as *The Saint, Department S, Randall & Hopkirk (Deceased)* and so on. I later drifted apart from Ray as he went off to America and carved himself quite a successful career, he then bought himself a title and became very grandiose. He seemed to forget his humble roots and workmates.

The series involved Shirley Logan (MacLaine), a globe-trotting magazine writer-photographer, and Dennis Croft (John Gregson), her London-based editor. It was one of the last projects John was involved in as, sadly, a few years later he died after suffering a heart attack, aged 54. He'd carved himself a very successful career in films such as *Battle of the River Plate, Genevieve* and *The Captain's Table* and was a thorough professional.

In the series, Shirley Logan found herself in all sorts of interesting situations. One of the most interesting was actually a real-life situation in Tokyo. We were out there on location and this particular Sunday morning my hotel telephone rang. "There's a student riot taking place and we want to get down there with a camera."

Quick as a flash, we dashed down into the city center with a handheld camera and Shirley MacLaine. Actually, we captured some pretty good footage—footage that would have cost a fortune had we had to stage such a demonstration. People later asked if it was at all dangerous; not that we really thought too much about it ourselves! In all honesty, the students were a pretty nice bunch but made a lot of noise!

Irene Handl

Next up was a TV spin-off movie. There was a very popular comedy series in 1970-71 called *For the Love of Ada* with Irene Handl and Wilfred Pickles. As was the trend then, it was decided that a movie should be made. To be honest, most movie spin-offs didn't really work, as they tried to stretch a 30 minute story, and 30-minute characters, into a full 90 minutes. But they were well-crafted pieces and good fun, and of course, gave people like me a few weeks of employment!

Ronnie Baxter directed—I think he directed some of the series too—and was a very nice chap. Both the leading players were super. Wilfred Pickles had been a big radio star and Irene Handl had worked her way through small roles in movies through to more substantial parts. She made so many films … over 100 I'd say, though mainly as supporting characters. Remember *I'm Alright Jack*, *The Italian Job* or *The Rebel*? She had that wonderful line in *The Rebel*, with Tony Hancock, when he—as a would-be artist—unveiled his masterpiece. "It's a self-portrait" he said proudly. "Who of?" she asked. Wonderful.

It was a nice little story of how these two characters had found each other in later life, and were now about to celebrate their first wedding anniversary; and they were unaware that their friends were planning a surprise party.

The nice thing about working with an experienced TV director like Ronnie was that he didn't hang about. TV shooting schedules are often very tight—remember, we had ten days to film *The Avengers* one-hour episodes. A feature of one hour would be at least twice that. It was much like the *Carry On* schedules, and that suited me fine as I then went off to do a *Carry On*—my first for a few years—with *Carry On Henry*, and then moved on to a very big production called *Zeppelin*.

Air Attacks

The outbreak of World War I places Scots officer Geoffrey Richter-Douglas (Michael York) in an uncomfortable position. Although his allegiance is to Britain, his mother was from an aristocratic Bavarian family, and he spent his summers in Germany as a child. When Geoffrey is approached by a German spy who offers him a chance to defect, he reports the incident to his superiors, but instead of arresting the spy they suggest that he accept her offer—and become an Allied agent. In Germany, among old friends, Geoffrey discovers that loyalty is more complicated than he expected, especially when he finds himself aboard the maiden voyage of a powerful new prototype zeppelin, headed for

Scotland on a secret mission that could decide the outcome of the war.

Hair-raising stuff. We filmed a lot over in Malta, as there is a sequence where the zeppelin is shot down over the sea, en route to Scotland, and it had to plunge into the water with all the actors in the personnel carriage underneath going with it. So that was all done on the water tank.

We filmed a lot coming up to Christmas time and it was very, very cold and wet. It started to rain and as the rain came down, everything froze—all the electric cables, the lamps—everything. If anyone touched anything, they'd get a shock and short things out. The producer came to me and said "we're getting behind schedule" and I explained that it was because we couldn't move things around very easily, as people kept getting electric shocks. He said, "Well, the director tells me that we're getting behind because you're so slow." Hang on a minute, I thought, that's a bit off. I told him to touch a lamp to see what I meant. He did and duly got a shock and shorted it out. I don't think he grumbled again.

There were lots of miniatures and models involved on this film, as you might expect. The guy in charge of those had also been in charge of the miniatures for the film *Battle of Britain*, a lovely guy named Wally Veevers. I didn't get too involved in that side of things, as they'd have a separate unit and camera team dedicated to the model unit. I was involved with one large model on the airfield in Malta, with the zeppelin coming out of a hangar. Generally, it's a slow process and that's why there is another unit dedicated—it would slow the main unit down so much that, financially, it would become too costly.

On some films there can be a number of film units working simultaneously: The main unit, the second unit (action sequences), a model unit and maybe even an underwater unit. It's one big logistical exercise with a number of cameramen, and of course the important thing is making everything match; and so the cameraman on each unit and I would have a chat, they'd see our rushes and get a feel for what we've done and how it looked. We'd always talk!

I then went from the cold into the hot—more precisely, fire.

Hot Hot Hot

The Firechasers was a TV film, directed by Sid Hayers, and it was a bit of a tough assignment actually because, as you might surmise, it involved a lot of fires. Keith Barron played an insurance investigator on the trail of arsonists.

There were lots of small-scale fires, but the big one—the climax—came when we set Brentford docks alight. Nowadays it's a marina with wonderfully expensive flats, but back then there were all sorts of warehouses and old buildings there. It was one of these old, three-story buildings that we set on fire. You've never seen such a fire in your life! There were jets and propane bottles everywhere. When I say we set it alight, I mislead you slightly. I should say, we created the illusion of it being alight thanks to some very clever special effects guys; though seeing it, you'd have thought it was really ablaze! In fact, many people in the locale did actually think it was a real fire, and dialed 999 calling for the fire brigade.

As with all controlled fires, we did actually have a few fire engines with us on the location ... just in case. The shoot lasted about ten minutes, I guess. I had a couple or even three cameras on it and in it, and we were actually inside the building. We had a scary moment when we were filming the last escape from the building. We were all in the basement and moved into the lift—Sid, myself and the camera operator and another—and we had to go up to the ground level. Meanwhile, the lift jammed halfway up. The fires were blazing and, of course, oxygen was not that plentiful. One of the chaps in the lift started to panic, and it all got a little hairy. Mercifully, the lift started up again within a few seconds, though it seemed like minutes, and we were out.

The blazing building was quite a sight to behold and it was, of course, night too, and so it looked even better!

After Sid was happy with the take, he called for the fire brigade guys to move in and extinguish everything safely. They shot an immense amount of water into the building as "simulated" fires are actually more difficult to put out than real fires. A little while later it was all deemed safe, though one thing we didn't anticipate was all of that water trickling down to ground level. It was night, and it was winter. The water froze! So you can imagine the sight of a film crew and all these fire brigade guys slipping and sliding around on ice.

Comedy Roots

It was nice to get back to Pinewood and move on to a lovely comedy film, directed by Gerry Thomas and produced by Peter Rogers. It was, like *For the Love of Ada,* a film spin-off of a successful TV series. In this case, *Bless This House.*

Of course, it was an ideal project for Gerry and Peter as the series starred Sid James and, with it, his familiar and popular brand of humor. Starring along with Sid was Diana Coupland and Sally Geeson. The part of Sid's son was re-cast. In the series it had been Robin Stewart, though I'd heard rumors that he was a bad time keeper and was often late for recordings, and so Peter didn't take any chances! He cast Robin

Askwith. Then another old chum came on board in the shape of Peter Butterworth as Sid's neighbor Trevor, Patsy Rowlands was his wife Betty (as she was the character's wife in the series) and two new neighbours, played by Terry Scott and June Whitfield, completed the main cast. It was just like a *Carry On* get-together.

Needless to say, it was the usual five-week schedule and based at Pinewood, plus exteriors around Windsor. It was great fun. As I've already mentioned, there seemed to be a trend of taking small-screen series and making a big-screen spin off in the '70s. Many misfired, but *Bless This House* was one of the successful ones. It wasn't just a case of spinning 30 minutes into 90. The original script by Dave Freeman was funny, the characters (and cast) worked well and there was just the right amount of risqué humour introduced to tap in to the successful *Carry On* market. Peter and Gerry had it off to a tee. One thought that it might have led to another *Bless This House* film, but Peter wasn't really that keen. He'd achieved good mileage from the characters and was satisfied. Some (other) producers did try though ... look at the feature spin-offs from *Steptoe* and *On the Buses*. The first was very funny, whereas sequels never quite hit the same mark. Interestingly, *On the Buses* was the most successful film made by Hammer Studios—yet it is for the horror films that they'll forever be remembered.

Olympics

Visions of Eight was an interesting project. This movie has eight of that era's top directors from around the world coming together with producer David L. Wolper, a renowned historian, to look at the 1972 Olympics through the camera's eyes. There follows a journey through eight different parts of the Olympics. I was DoP of the segment called *The Fastest* for director Kon Ichikawa. My old mate Arthur Wooster did *The Longest* for John Schlesinger. It was a hair-raising time in Munich as the Israeli living quarters were shot-up; they were troubled times as they still are now in the Far East. Whilst having breakfast on the eighth floor of my hotel, I saw all these helicopters come in full of troops. Not the best sort of environment to start the day off in.

Anyway, I was filming the sequence of when the flame arrived at the stadium, with the athlete running holding it in the air. He ran up loads of steps to the big bowl and my camera panned with him every inch of the way. I was actually holding the camera and after a few minutes began to feel the weight, and whilst I managed to maintain a steady hand my legs were shaking like jelly! Then, up at the back of the big bowl, now lit up, came this crane platform; as it rose I could see

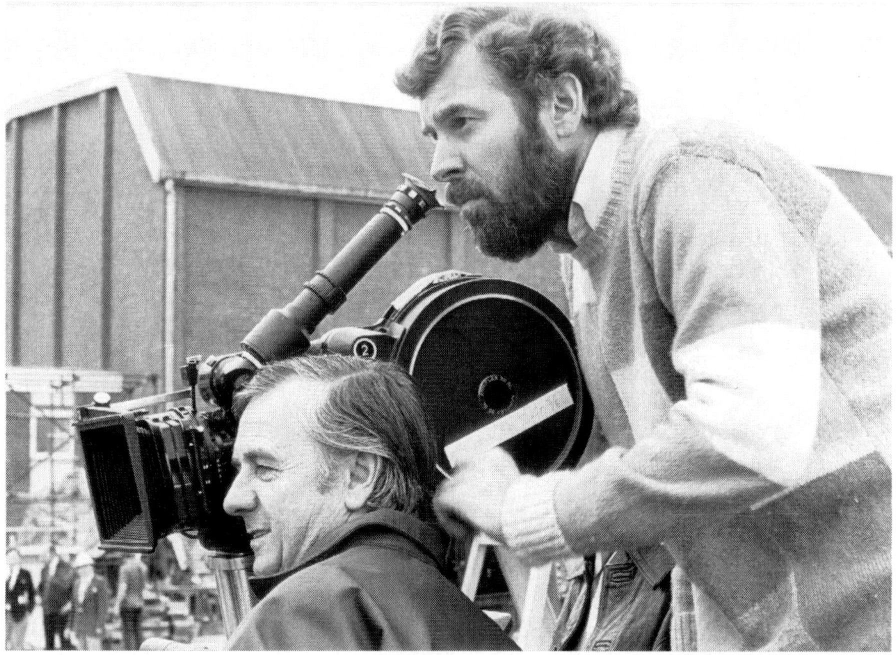

Top: Chaos on the streets with *Shirley's World* (Alan on handheld camera)
Bottom: Alan with Kevin Connor—starting many years of happy association.

Arthur on it with his camera! He wanted a shot of the stadium with the flame in the foreground, but was ruining my shot. I signalled to him on the radio and he said "See you later." As the platform went down. Arthur held his nose as though going under water. It was so funny.

A few minutes later he reappeared, covered in branches and leaves. He thought it wouldn't be so bad in my shot if he was camouflaged! It was hilarious. But it turned out to be a fascinating and critically acclaimed documentary. I'm quite pleased of my little contribution!

Not Now

I returned to comedy for my next film, *Not Now Darling*. It was the film adaptation of a successful London farce by Ray Cooney and John Roy Chapman. Cooney co-directed (and co-starred too) the film farce with David Croft, who was famous for directing TV shows such as *It Ain't Alf Hot Mum, Are You Being Served?* and *Dad's Army*. David was red hot on screen direction whereas Ray was good on farce, and so they complimented each other beautifully and worked very well. It's just a shame the material wasn't a bit stronger.

The cast was a who's who of British comedy: Leslie Phillips, Joan Sims, Barbara Windsor, Bill Fraser, Peter Butterworth, Graham Stark and so on.

The only thing of note I remember was that we shot in "Multivista" format. It's a shoot-and-edit process much like that used in TV taping when you have one set. It wasn't very satisfactory I'm afraid and the overall look doesn't really lift the piece.

It was followed a few years later by *Not Now Comrade*, though I wasn't involved, with much of the same key crew and cast.

Kevin

My next film began a collaboration which lasted for many happy years with a young director named Kevin Connor. Kevin had made his name as an editor of feature films, notably with Richard Attenborough. Like a lot of other editors, he yearned to try his hand at directing.

He became friendly with a producer named John Dark, and together they set up a company and set about financing some projects. The first to come to fruition was a terrific horror film, *From Beyond the Grave* for Warners. Milton Subotsky was one of the producers (and that too was the start of a long collaboration with Kevin).

It was an anthology film for Amicus. I started the chapter with them, and I'll end it too.

The film was the adaptation of four short stories by R Chetwynd-Hayes, all hinging around an old antique shop owner and the fate that befalls the customers who try to cheat him.

What a cast! Peter Cushing played the old antique shop owner, and then came Ian Bannen, Ian Carmichael, Diana Dors, Donald Pleasence, Nyree Dawn Porter, David Warner, Ian Ogilvy, Lesley-Anne Down and loads of others. I guess it was a fairly quiet time in the British Film Industry and so we were terrifically fortunate that these people were all available. It was nice having four stories too, as it meant they'd only be needed for a couple or three weeks. An appealing thought for an actor between jobs. Okay, it wasn't the 'starring' role, but a good one and great fun.

I found Kevin to be a wonderful director. He knew exactly what he wanted and you could tell that he was editing it in his head as he shot. Like Gerry Thomas, he didn't hang around or waste time thinking about set-ups. We shot this film out of Shepperton, "The Gate Crasher" was about a charmed mirror letting loose an evil spirit. In "An Act of Kindness," an ex-military officer gets entangled with the occult. The third episode, "The Elemental," sees a wealthy couple plagued by a demon. The final tale, "The Door," involves a magic door which leads to another dimension.

The good thing about directors who have risen through the ranks of the editing rooms; like Gerry Thomas, John Glen and Kevin Connor, is that they have the invaluable ability of knowing what coverage to shoot. For example, an inexperienced director who has a 3-minute scene might choose to shoot it all in one take, with a medium shot. So he has no close-ups, long shots or cutaways. Now that really restricts the editor, as he has nothing to use. Editing is very important in emphasizing certain points in the story, or characters, or in building suspense and setting the pace. They always say that good editing can save a bad film, and bad editing can destroy a good one. But then, the editor can only work with what the director gives him or her.

That's why I always found it very useful to sit in rushes and watch footage we'd shot the previous day. The director would sit making suggestions to the editor, and we'd all get a feel for the way it was going. Some directors choose to shot the whole film before they sit down and start the editing process. I think it's far better to edit as the film is in production, as normally within a few days of finishing the shoot, we have a rough cut to look at. And along the way, if something doesn't quite work or we need an extra shot, it's far easier (and less expensive) to do it whilst you still have the unit together. Calling them back for re-shoots when filming has finished and we've all gone our separate ways can be very expensive. Sometimes it is necessary as with *A Fish Called Wanda* which I will come to a little later, but generally not a good idea!

VII

Confession of a Lighting Cameraman

I stayed in the horror genre—after completing *Carry On Girls*—for *The Legend of Hell House*. That was directed by a young guy named John Hough.

John is a very interesting chap. He started off working on the TV action shows like *The Saint* and *The Baron*. He wasn't a director then, but he approached the producer and asked how much it cost to run the second unit for a day. The reply was something like £400 (for the sake of argument) and so this young chap said, "okay, you let me direct the second unit for a day and if I bugger it up, I'll pay the £400." They did, and he didn't. It was the start of a very interesting career for young John.

He made a few films before this, including *Treasure Island* with Orson Welles and a couple of horror thrillers. I guess he was making a bit of a name for himself in the genre.

Hell House was based on a novel by Richard Matheson and produced by one of *The Avengers* producers, Albert Fennell, with whom John enjoyed a long and fruitful professional relationship. We had the wonderful Roddy McDowall, Clive Revill, Roland Culver, Peter Bowles, Michael Gough and Pamela Franklin in the cast. It was all about four people arriving at a haunted house where, previously, a number of psychic investigators had been killed. Spooky stuff.

Clive Revill was the physicist who tries to clear the house of evil; Pamela Franklin a medium; and Roddy McDowall the survivor of a previous incursion. Shock value played a significant element, and I think we achieved it wonderfully with good camera movement, lighting and some good editing by Geoffrey Foot.

John was a very inventive director with good ideas. He was a strong character. I think he did an excellent job and the overall film looked slick and had all the right elements in the right places—when the audience were supposed to jump, they jumped! One critic went as far as to call it "one of the most absorbing, goose-fleshing and mind-pleasing ghost breaker yarns on film."

John went on to direct a few films for Disney after this, including one with Bette Davis, and despite the success he's had in maintaining a career directing movies and TV shows, I'm sorry he didn't make it really big. He had the talent and enthusiasm, but I guess it was a tough time in the business and just to be working was something. Had the industry been a bit busier in the '70s with more films on offer, I think John would have done better than he has. That's not in any way disrespectful, but he had a talent that wasn't really capitalized upon as it might have been.

Forgetfulness

It wasn't long before I was working with Kevin Connor and John Dark again. It was 1975, and *The Land That Time Forgot.* Terrific. This was Amicus's high adventure and action in prehistoric times. In a way, it was a forerunner to the Indiana Jones films. It had that style.

Doug McClure starred with John McEnery, Susan Penhaligon and Keith Barron. It was based on Edgar Rice Burroughs' novel.

The elements that really grabbed me on this were the wonderful sets. I hadn't seen anything like them before. It was all due to a wonderful production designer, Maurice Carter. He was—like the rest of the crew—a joy to work with. Sadly he is no longer with us, though his family are still in the film business as his daughter, Diana Hawkins, produces with Richard Attenborough.

I wouldn't get too involved in the design process myself, especially with someone as experienced as Maurice, but I would be around to discuss any ideas or doubts they might have about, for instance, shooting in a large set with lots of bubbling water and smoke. I'd need to insure I had certain vantage points to set up my camera and capture all the action without restriction. Maurice was very good like that. He always thought about the camera when designing. Walls would be movable; ceiling pieces too, if required. Some designers just want to be extravagant and show off what they can do. Great. But if the camera can't move around as the director would like, what's the point?

I've always found that the more experienced a crew or key individuals are within that crew, then the more receptive they are to ideas and suggestions. Would I therefore, you might ask, turn down work when there were "new" boys in charge? No, not at all. I always held the belief that I could work with anyone and that nothing is impossible. Sometimes it might take a little longer, but it's never impossible. Having said that, there are probably a few people I wouldn't care to work with (or work with again)—well-known people—and thankfully I've never had to take a job I didn't want to, purely for the money. As I've already mentioned, I've worked with directors who have come from the theater, and they relied on me for the technical side of directing, with the camera and lights, and that can be very fulfilling. So no, that's never really been a factor.

On this film, I remember we had the giant silent stage at Shepperton, which has a water tank incorporated, and you can flood the entire stage to a depth of about six feet. We did! We had to as it was all set during World War I, when a German U-boat sinks a British ship and takes the survivors on board. After taking a wrong turn, the submarine takes them to the unknown land of Caprona, where they find dinosaurs and Neanderthals.

Much of the special effects fell to a very talented young chap named Derek Meddings. Sadly he is no longer with us, but boy, did he leave a legacy. Derek was a very likable sort of guy, very unassuming, and nothing was too much trouble. He started out in the business with Gerry and Sylvia Anderson on some of their marionette shows such as *Thunderbirds* and *Fireball XL5*. I think this was only his third or fourth film.

Now, the budget wasn't limitless and technology wasn't, in all fairness, that far advanced. So yes, looking at the film today it might appear a little "basic" when it comes to the models and effects, but for its time it was bloody marvelous. Derek went on to some big films, including several Bonds, and won the Oscar for *Superman*. He made Superman fly!

Another important chap I must mention here is a true legend. You might not know his name, but without him special effects and photography would not be as advanced as it is today. His name was Charles "Charlie" Staffell. Charlie started out in the business in the early 1940s and was still working in 1999. His last film was Kubrick's last film, *Eyes Wide Shut*.

Projection

Charlie developed the back and front projection process and special photography (e.g., split screen) to near perfection. In fact, he was the first technical person to win an Oscar for services to the film industry. He did everything from *Batman* and *Aliens* to Bond. What a guy.

Back and front projection techniques are whereby an actor stands in front of a screen, and the background is artificially created or, in this case, projected. Nowadays you'll be more used to seeing "blue screen" or "green screen" techniques used and computers generating images. Charlie paved the way for all that.

Fittingly, his Oscar and Derek Meddings' stand side by side at Pinewood Studios. A fitting memorial to the great men.

As you've probably gathered by now, I was never far away from a comedy. Next up was *Confessions of a Pop Performer*. Oh yes!

If you thought the *Carry On* films were saucy, then this was double–X-rated sauce!!

A young producer by the name of Greg Smith hit upon the idea of this series of *Confessions* films. There were four in all. He'd seen the *Carry On* films, and I guess saw the potential for slightly bawdier films, with a few more "tits and bums" if you'll forgive the expression; and that's just what these stories offered. The first was *Confessions of a Window Cleaner*. It was co-scripted and directed by Val Guest, though he all but forgets to mention it nowadays, and after the lead role of Timothy Lea was turned down by Nicky Henson, Dennis Waterman and Richard Beckinsale, it went to a young Robin Askwith who had, coincidentally, just completed an advert as a young sex-charged window cleaner.

Surprisingly, it attracted a considerable cast: Anthony Booth, Dandy Nicholls, Bill Maynard, John Le Mesurier, Joan Hickson and Richard Wattis.

It did rather well at the box office and spawned a sequel. The one I did. We had much the same cast, though a different director in Norman Cohen. One of the reviews compared it to "the average German sex comedy." I didn't know if that was good or bad!

Our lead character gives up being a window cleaner and, instead, joins a rock group. Hence the title.

In a way, they were competing with the *Carry On*s in so much as it was mainly the same audience. They were very risqué and, as a result, the *Carry On*s became that bit more risqué too, especially *Emmannuelle* in 1978. That was the last in the series … until 1992. They made two more *Confessions* films, *Driving Instructor* and *From a Holiday Camp*. I guess I must have been busy elsewhere though, as I never did another, despite being asked.

Blaxploitation

I did however work on the sequel to *Cleopatra Jones*, called *Cleopatra Jones and the Casino of Gold*. The first of the two was made in 1973, at the height of the blaxploitation films, with movies such as *Shaft* hitting screens. *Cleopatra Jones* didn't quite measure up in the box office stakes. In a way I suppose that she was supposed to be the female Shaft. It didn't quite work. Cleopatra Jones was a United States Special Agent assigned to crack down on drug-trafficking in the U.S. and abroad.

The first one was quite weird, even by '70s standards! Tamara Dobson (Jones) was a very good-looking black woman, but it was said Cleopatra couldn't really "kick butt" because she'd mess up her outlandish '70s fashions, including big furry hats and tight dresses with spangles!

However, the money men commissioned another and so *Casino of Gold* moved into production in Hong Kong in 1974. When I arrived out there, the director (who shall remain nameless) was all set and raring to go. However, four days into the shoot he was fired. I'm not in a position to comment as to why; speculation was that he fell out with the producer. We'll leave it at that. It was then announced that Chuck Bail was coming out from America to replace him.

On his first day, he called the key crew together—myself, the operator, the editor, production manager and so on—and laid his cards on the table. He made no bones about it.

"Look, guys, I'm taking over the picture. Mr. so-and-so has left the film and now I'm here. I'm a stunt man and action director, I've directed one film before this called *Black Samson* but I'm going to need your help on this one."

With that, he had everyone 100 percent. He wasn't at all pretentious or a "know it all" and it really cemented a terrific working relationship. True, the film and script weren't that fantastic, but it was well-crafted and, as always, great fun. Tamara Dobson played the lead again; she hadn't done much before (or since) but was very professional. Shooting conditions were tricky, because as soon as you put a camera down on the street for a location set-up you'd have two or three hundred people gathering around, and you could never move them on! That was very annoying at times. The studio work was mostly done at Shaw Brothers, and they had good film people there—set builders, electricians and so on. Well, they had been making a lot of martial arts films there, amongst others, and so the infrastructure was developing. I took my camera operator and assistant from London, as it was important to me that I have people I had worked with before and that there wasn't a language barrier perhaps! Panavision had a rental house out there, and so the camera equipment wasn't a problem, it was all bang up-to-date stuff. There was also a very good processing laboratory, so rushes came through the next morning. They really couldn't do enough for us.

I remember another little funny story. There were lots of local crew on this film, and sometimes the language barrier got in the way. I know this one particular day we were due on location at 8 A.M. But there was a major cock-up and the props people, along with some others, went to the wrong location. It delayed things a fair while. As such, the production manager called a meeting at lunch time. He was a lovely guy! At this meeting he said "I've called you all together to point out that there have been several instances where production has been hindered, and there have been problems—particularly with the prop department. In future, I want you all on the correct location at eight-o-clock-o and no fucking-up-o!"

He'd mastered the language! But I would add that, actually, there were all on time in the future.

It was financed by Warner Bros and I often recall a "big cheese" around the set. Perhaps anxious about getting it right with the second director! They probably had a lot of money tied up in the film, and it was quite far away from home in Hollywood to risk not having a set of eyes and ears around the set.

You might be asking, why was a British cinematographer working on an American film with an American director in Hong Kong? It seems slightly odd maybe, but you must remember that British lighting cameramen were hailed as the best in the world. I don't dare put myself anywhere up there, but by virtue of being a Brit and having a good body of work behind me, I got the call. I also knew Warner's London man (through working with John Dark), Paul Hitchcock. I believe Paul had a lot to do in setting up the picture in Hong Kong as he had with John Dark's *From Beyond the Grave*. He's since gone to great heights in the business as an executive producer on films such as *Mission Impossible I* and *II*, *The Man in the Iron Mask* and *The Saint*.

Chuck meanwhile later went on to direct a lot of television such as *CHiPs*, *Knight Rider* and *Baywatch Nights*. Great success I wish him too, as he was terrific to work with, and unlike some I could mention, he did work *with* you. Bizarrely, the film was banned in Sweden and the Netherlands.

Swords and Lances

Next it was back to work with my old mate Kevin Connor. It wasn't set in prehistoric days this time, it was a contemporary piece, though with a touch of the medieval all the same.

Trial By Combat starred John Mills, Donald Pleasence and Peter Cushing. It was supposedly inspired by the style of *The Avengers*, with a touch of the comic macabre.

Top: Inside the giant drill, our dapper heroes prepare for a whole new world. *Bottom:* The exciting opening sequence from *At the Earth's Core* where Peter Cushing and Doug McClure tunnel towards the center of the Earth.

Doug McClure and Cy Grant are heading for trouble at the core.

A group of British aristocrats, who call themselves "Knights of Avalon," aren't happy with the British justice system and take it upon themselves to provide real justice. However, instead of just killing the people they believe guilty, they give them a chance in traditional combat. This is their trial.

When one day Sir Edward Gifford (Peter Cushing) witnesses one of their trials, they have to "remove" him too. His son and heir, Sir John from America (David Birney), starts to investigate with help from Marion Evans (Barbara Hershey) and Colonel Cook (John Mills) from Scotland Yard. It's all good stuff, a bit eccentric maybe, but believable.

We had a few horses on this film. I hadn't worked a tremendous amount with them before this time, and whilst not exactly worried you do always have that tiny element of doubt implanted about how they might behave—especially when they have all the dressing on for the jousting scenes. The horses—and riders—had trained for a number of weeks though, and rehearsed the sequences meticulously. In fact, I don't recall an incident where anything went wrong or didn't quite work as planned. We were very lucky. In fact, despite shooting night sequences, and dawn sequences and locations in Kent, we came in on a six-week schedule. Everyone was happy, the picture did well, and Kevin and I moved on to yet another film together. That was *At the Earth's Core.*

Core

It was nice to see Doug McClure back, and dear Peter Cushing too. They headed the cast on a Victorian-set adventure yarn. Doug was really beginning to make a name for himself as a good leading man. He'd clocked up 30-odd film credits by now and was a true joy to work with. As indeed was Peter Cushing. He'd had a run of horror films before *Trial By Combat* and *At The Earth's Core*, and so I think he really enjoyed playing a somewhat eccentric professor alongside Doug McClure. Whilst his wonderful gaunt looks and drawn face was so perfect for horror films, a pair of spectacles and umbrella transformed him in to a lovable grandfather character. Terribly British too, naturally. His umbrella assisted in many scrapes with the prehistoric monsters. Ah yes, we were back playing with them again!

The story is set, as mentioned, in Victorian times when two geologists (McClure and Cushing) are preparing to test out "the Iron mole" a giant earth-boring drill contraption. Down into a Welsh hillside they go, but then something goes wrong. They head towards the Earth's core, thought to be molten rock, and therefore they're drilling towards certain death. But no! Far from it. They land in the underground cavernous world of Pellucidar, where prehistoric bird-like creatures rule and humans are slaves. It was a take on the *Planet of the Apes* story … or rather, Pierre Boulle (the author of *Apes*) *did* a take on this Edgar Rice Burroughs story!

A love interest is introduced in the shape of Caroline Munro. Doug's character falls for her, and, needless to say, she ends up in trouble and he must risk his life to save her.

Kevin kept the direction straightforward, but maintained a good balance of humor throughout. It was great fun working with all the creatures. They were pretty scary, let me tell you, though looking at the film nowadays I guess kids wouldn't think so. It's pretty tame compared to some of the stuff they see nowadays. The majority, if not all, of the effects were created "in camera." That is to say, we did very little after shooting. We had various projection techniques, models and miniatures but there were certainly no computers around or the chance to "fix it in post-production" if we didn't capture it on the stage floor.

It was interesting lighting this picture. After all, we were supposed to be in the center of the earth, so it would be pretty dark, wouldn't it? Well, in reality, yes, but then again without light, life would not be sustained down there so we had to use a little creative license or it would all be ridiculous. I did try for an eerie, unnatural "reddish" lighting look. A few filters, subdued lighting and correct focus and concentration of lighting did the trick. It's no good having scenes with actors so dark that you're straining to see them, and after all the producer is paying them a good salary to be there so he wants to see them. So you have to light them to their best, whilst bearing in mind the surroundings and "natural" light in the world we created. In the final show-down with the horrible bird creatures, that was all underground, and so I could "turn down" the lights a little. That helped with the models too—they were good, but not overly brilliant in flight, so the less light on them the better, really. Like all of Kevin's Rice Burroughs pictures, we did marvels on the budgets and schedules. There's a few more to talk about, but before those I was asked to work abroad in Africa on a big action picture that Peter Hunt was directing. Rousing stuff!

The Devil and John Glen

Shout at the Devil was a terrific Wilbur Smith story which producer Michael Klinger had bought the rights—I think he purchased the rights to a number of Smith stories, in fact, as a couple of years earlier he'd filmed *Gold* (based on the novel *Goldmine*) with Roger Moore and Susannah York, directed by Peter Hunt. *Devil* starred Roger Moore and Lee Marvin as upper-class Sebastian Oldsmith and Irish rogue Flynn O'Flynn respectively. A tale of ivory poaching, smuggling and the beginnings of World War I.

I was hired in on the second-unit crew with John Glen, who was directing, as DoP. We were really in charge of all the action sequences that took a bit of time to set up, as obviously you couldn't have the main unit (with all the expensive actors) hanging around too much whilst sequences are arranged.

If you've seen the film you'll remember the old two-seater Vickers Vimmy aeroplane which Roger's character uses to recce an area, looking for a German battleship which had put in for repair under camouflage. Well, it was quite a dodgy little machine to say the least, but they had a great South African stunt pilot, Nick Turvey. He flew this thing around and did a few tricky bits of maneuvering in through valleys and channels, and caused me to feel a bit queasy. Why, you ask? Well, it was muggings here who was in the front (gunner) seat of the plane with the camera, filming all ways to capture the action up the Ozumbuvue river where this battleship is holed up. On one of the many approaches we made up the river, the engine pitch changed considerably and sounded as though it was changing down gears … until the power went altogether and we ended up in the river. The "emergency services" were there on the spot, and within seconds everyone was taken to safety and the plane floated on special floats they had made, before it was taken ashore and prepped to fly again! The problem was, we discovered, was that the driving mechanism to the propeller was connected via a series of pulley wheels and belts, and it was these belts that were breaking. I guess a combination of the weight (with the camera) and the stress the machine was under in doing all of the "stunt" flying took its toll. It was soon fixed up again and airborne. But again, at a crucial moment, the damn engine pitch would change and we knew what was coming … water! It wasn't very satisfactory and it was after this that John said he had an idea. He'd decided to hire a more reliable plane—a crop sprayer I believe—which would physically tow our Vickers!

There were a few big set pieces in that picture, not least the final one when they blew up the Blucher. They really did blow it up! I'll never

On location with Roger Moore and Lee Marvin during *Shout at the Devil*, showing support for Alan's favorite soccer team!

forget the noise and smoke. We'd spent all morning laying down a thick fog over the river and what with that, exhaust fumes from the various boats and then the explosion ... blimey, you've never seen anything like it in your life.

Peter Hunt was the main unit director on the picture, and he had of course much experience of these types of action movies through his work on the Bond films and the aforementioned *Gold.* He was a lovely man, with a great sense of humor. I knew him pretty well before this film as he was a friend of my brother Kenneth. It was really through him that John Glen and I were invited to join the picture, and thus it started a working relationship with John and I that lasted many years and, indeed, a friendship that has extended to this day. It was with Peter's help that I got my break on the Bond films later on, with John. I'll forever be grateful to him for that. It's amazing how things work out, as it was only through John getting a job—as a teenager—in the cutting rooms at Shepperton, after a guy at Walton on Thames studios told him to try the Middlesex studio as there was nothing doing in Walton, that he got to know Peter through running errands in the editing department and subsequently working his way up through the ranks. You see, you just never know ... you meet someone, strike up a good rapport, and then 20-odd years later you receive a phone call offering you a job which leads to even greater riches.

However, there were tensions between Peter and the producer, Michael Klinger, on the picture, primarily over the budget I think. I steered clear, but John got embroiled in it all. He was supposed to be second unit director and editor, but they'd kept him (and me) in South Africa setting up a sequence with a crocodile that was to attack Flynn after he staggered from the wreck of the Blucher at the end of the film. We spent ages trying various ways to shoot this, whilst the main unit moved to Malta, and just as we thought we had it the call came to recall John to Malta and abort the sequence. For some reason he was then told that his assistant would be cutting the film and his services were more or less redundant. Peter seemed very cold towards John, and after at a crew screening when John called Peter to offer his thoughts on the film, he was more or less told that they were not welcome.

I suspect that Peter believed John to be on Michael Klinger's "side" and felt betrayed. It was all nonsense, of course.

We worked a lot in South Africa on this picture, in terrible heat and quite basic conditions—when compared to the comfort of one's home base. But it was a great unit, and both Roger and Lee Marvin really lifted spirits (quite literally at times—to their lips!) and made it fun. We were working in the Transkei, where troubles with apartheid were visible brewing, before the area changed to Black rule, so it was all a great education to me.

VIII

Amsterdam and Atlantis

The Wombles was very successful on television. A children's favorite. It came in bursts of five-minute episodes, all voiced beautifully by Bernard Cribbins.

I'm not sure whether the idea of making a film came before involving Lionel Jeffries, or whether it was an idea he had and developed a script for. It isn't a film he welcomes talking about, so I can't tell you. What I can tell you is that, many years after pulling out of film financing, the Rank Organization made a big splash about a new program of exciting films, and *Wombling Free* was the first of them. It did attract a few strange looks and comments in Wardour Street. The powers-that-be had spoken, though, and it was given the green light.

The four-foot high furry creatures who dwell under Wimbledon Common, collecting and recycling rubbish, were—in the TV series—invisible to humans, and as such we never really saw any storylines featuring humans. But that was the center to this story. David Tomlinson, Frances de la Tour and a young Bonnie Langford played the humans, and the Wombles had to enlist their support to save Wimbledon Common from being developed into a housing estate, thus meaning the Wombles were in danger of losing their home and way of life.

Rather than bring the little furry creatures to life with puppetry and animation, we had to do it "for real." Therefore all sorts of little furry suits and costumes were made, and of course only people who were of a certain height could be cast to fill the suits. That was a big expense and very uncomfortable. After ten minutes in the suits, they found it too hot to carry on; breathing was difficult too. It was tricky for them to see where they were going. And so we had a number of limitations imposed on us straight away. The underground tunnel sets had to be build to that smaller scale too, which is okay for them but when you have a full-sized crew and lighting, cameras, etc. again you have limitations.

I think all this took its toll on Lionel. He maintained that the producer, Ian Shand, kept interfering too and that led to tension between them. Lionel, too, was fresh from a big success with *The Railway Children* and did have a manner of "knowing it all," you might say. I kept my head down and got on with the job, but you can't help but notice the tensions and ill-feeling, and whilst I'm a happy-go-lucky sort of chap and let it all go over my head, there were others who were not so fortunate. I know David Tomlinson wasn't happy. In fact, in his autobiography he totally skips this film, just mentioning it in the filmography.

There were some lovely sets and costumes on the picture and, it looked high-quality. At the cinema it fared poorly. Critics were harsh and it didn't go in to profit.

Amazingly, though, they left one of the main sets on the stage at Pinewood after the filming had ended. When the studio MD asked why, he was staggered. "We're using it for *Wombling Free 2*," was the response. Needless to say, it never happened and the set was soon struck (or dismantled, to give it the non-filmy description!).

Gulliver

I next received a call from Peter Hunt. Obviously he didn't hold any grudges against me, saying that he was about to start on a film of *Gulliver's Travels* and would I like to join him? Of course I would!

Richard Harris was Gulliver and the only human in the story, as the Lilliputians were all animated. The animation was done in Brussels whilst the live action was filmed at Pinewood. The animation was pretty much in place, and we had very heavy storyboarding with Richard. It worked surprisingly well, actually.

Richard was terrific to work with. I knew he had a bit of a reputation as difficult and a "hellraiser," but on set he was totally professional. I recall one day we had him flat on his back, tied up. He must have been there for two or three hours and never mumbled a word of complaint. It just goes to show that a lot of stories about artists and their behavior are not always to be believed.

I guess I was on the picture for about six weeks. It was pretty fast, but then again I suppose with the live action we were just filling in gaps in the animation. So a six-week shoot for us may well have transferred into a six- or twelve-month one for the animators.

Sadly, it didn't do great business and I think some of the reviews were a bit harsh. It was a lovely children's story and I think it looked very good from an artistic standpoint. About 20 years later, Channel 4 made another version, though all live action. That was very good, but of course technology had advanced significantly too and a lot more was possible, as indeed has been demonstrated in the photography for *Lord of the Rings*.

Mitchum

By way of contrast, my next project in 1977 was a film called *The Amsterdam Kill* starring Robert Mitchum. What a guy he was. I'd seen a lot of his films over the years—he made about 150—and in years just prior to this picture he'd made *Ryan's Daughter* and *Midway*, so was riding on a bit of a high. I suppose maybe that accounted for him being a bit difficult in terms of demands he made on the production. Little things like wanting a mobile dressing room. Sounds simple but there weren't really many of these sorts of things readily available and I remember we were in a foreign land on location too. The production manager resorted to renting a lovely coach and it was modified to include everything—a shower, seating, mini-bar, etc.—and drove it out to the location and parked it up. They told him it was there, and he said he'd check it out later. And it was ages later that he did condescend to have a look at it: He walked in, said "Okay," walked out and never set foot in or near it again! He didn't really want, nor need, it. He just wanted to flex his muscles and stamp his feet. Well, that doesn't always work out in one's favor, I have discovered during my years in the business, and I think that did him a lot of harm actually—not only with the cast and crew on this film, but in terms of him developing a reputation as being difficult. For example, lots of producers putting a film together would probably say, if Mitchum's name was mentioned as a possible candidate for a part, "Why don't we call the producer or director of his last film and see what the word is?" It's common practice. So they call Mr. So-and-So and mention Mitchum; the response is "Oh, he's a difficult sod to work with, and demands this, that and the other...." It would make me think twice, to say the least!

Okay, it may have been a one off with Mitchum perhaps being in a bad mood one day (well, there was more to it from what I could see), but you're only as good as your last film, as they say, and indeed as good as your last "reference."

When you look at Mitchum's later credits, there aren't that many outstanding titles there. I won't say any more.

This particular film had backers from Hong Kong and it was written and directed by Robert Clouse, who had made a lot of action movies; he was famous for directing the Bruce Lee film *Enter The Dragon*. Mitchum played ex–DEA officer Quinlan, who was kicked out because he "made use" of some confiscated drug money … but then one of the leaders of an Amsterdam cartel wants out and thinks he can enlist Quinlan's help to tip off the DEA about drug deals, thus one by one turning-in the cartel members to the authorities. But it doesn't quite go according to plan, to say the least. It was quite a fast-paced picture, lots of action going on and of course nice locations in Holland and Hong Kong!

I enjoyed the experience and, as I've said before, I keep my head down and get on with it so I'm quite unaffected by any tension between actors and the bosses. But ultimately I suppose it does have a trickle-down effect and us boys on the floor might end up with a grumpy actor. But there we are—I've lived through worse!

More Forgetfulness

My next films were with my old mates Kevin Connor and John Dark. I suppose they were on a bit of a roll as they'd made a success out of their Doug McClure pictures and there was obviously a market for more. And so a sequel to *The Land That Time Forgot* was put into production, called *The People That Time Forgot*. It was much the same formula, though Doug wasn't the lead in this as the story was that his character had "dis-

Peter Gilmore and Doug McClure head the cast in *Warlords of Atlantis*.

Doug McClure discusses tactics with Shane Rimmer in *Warlords of Atlantis.*

appeared." A search party was set out to find him; Patrick (son of John) Wayne played the male lead Major McBride, and Doug did have a guest role in the picture as, ultimately, they found him in this prehistoric land beyond the arctic ice. Though, alas, not all of them made it out alive! You'll have to watch the film to see who did.

We had a great bunch of actors in that one. Thorley Walters, who had been a big name in comedy films in the '50s and '60s—(particularly with the Boulting Brothers), Tony Britton and Shane Rimmer. Providing the beauty were Sarah Douglas and Dana Gillespie.

Much of the behind-the-scenes gang were familiar faces to me. Maurice Carter designed the production again and there was a real family feel. I think that was a great bonus as when you're on a tight schedule, and limited budget, you don't have chance to drag your heels or mess up. The good thing about Kevin was that he'd surround himself by people he enjoyed working with and as a result they knew exactly how each other would think. So time was never wasted.

Atlantis

From this we went on to *Warlords of Atlantis,* a terrific action yarn set in Victorian England. Doug McClure was the star and in support were

Peter Gilmore, Lea Brodie, Shane Rimmer and Michael Gothard. One of the "minor" supporting actors, a crew hand, was John Ratzenberger, who went on, of course, to international fame as Cliff the postman in the comedy series *Cheers*. Like Shane Rimmer, he carved out a pretty regular work routine in Europe, as they were both North American, well Shane is Canadian actually, but they were here at a time when I guess there weren't that many jobbing American actors and so were pretty much in demand for a steady stream of films. John was in *Arabian Adventure* which I'll come to next (as was Shane), and a couple of *Superman* movies, not to mention a *Star Wars* too. I know John Dark and Kevin were keen to have an international feel and appeal to their films, and so they'd mix American with European actors. As a result, the films played well in all sorts of countries.

It was a typical "good vs. evil" story; Searching for the lost world of Atlantis, Prof. Aitken (Gilmore), his son Charles and Greg Collinson (McClure) are betrayed by the crew of their expedition's ship, attracted by the fabulous treasures of Atlantis. The diving bell destroyed, a deep sea monster attacks the boat. They are all dragged to the bottom of the sea where they meet the inhabitants of the lost continent, an advanced alien race that makes slaves of the ship wrecked sailors. The aliens want to rule the human world to create a dictator state. Due to his high IQ, they think that Charles may join them. Greg and the team enlist the help of Delphine (Lea Brodie), the daughter of a slave, to escape the city surrounded by evil creatures.

There was a great mixture of front projection techniques and model work involved. Charlie Staffell was in charge of project, and Cliff Culley worked with him as matte artist, creating scenery and locations that weren't really there—or indeed, if they *were* there, he exaggerated and improved them!

As there was lots of sea and water material to film, a second unit was employed to work on that side of things. My old friend Arthur Wooster being the man in charge, developed himself a terrific reputation for being an excellent second unit director and photographer. Again, he worked on many of the Bond films and then on films such as *The Avengers, Enigma, From Hell* and *The Count of Monte Cristo*. A lot of the work Arthur did on this film was out in Malta on the exterior tank, which was handy as I think we were filming off Majorca for some of the volcanic island locations (La Palma), with black coal dust everywhere. So the second unit wasn't too far away.

John Richardson was involved in the special effects. He was a terrific guy who had followed his father, Cliff, into the business. John later went on to win the Oscar for *Aliens* and is always busy. In addition to numerous James Bond films, he also added the magic to the Harry

Potter films. He worked alongside George Gibbs and a chap named Roger Dickens, who created the various monsters in the film—including the great octopuss that attacks the boat. Looking at it now, it looks a little creaky, but you must remember this was long before CGI effects and we had a pretty tight budget. All of the effects were physically achieved with models and miniatures and pretty much as we were shooting, so there wasn't the luxury of doing it in post-production, or letting it go wrong for that matter. A lot was achieved on the water stage at Shepperton too, which suited me fine as being an indoor tank, it gave a certain amount more control. If it rained outside, it didn't affect us.

No sooner had we completed *Warlords* before the next Dark-Connor film was put in to pre-production, *Arabian Adventure*. It was a mixture of magic carpets, and nasty villains *a la The Thief of Bagdad*. Christopher Lee, Oliver Tobias, Mickey Rooney, Milo O'Shea, Elizabeth Welch, Peter Cushing ... it really was an all-star cast.

Flying Carpets

I was thrilled to meet Mickey Rooney as I'd almost grown up with him at the cinema with his Andy Hardy films. He was terrific, and a really nice personality. I think within half an hour we'd heard his life story. Milo O'Shea was full of the typical Irish charm.

The young girl in the film was Emma Samms. This was her first film, and there was quite a battle to get her. I know Kevin met many young hopefuls in auditions, but he didn't feel any of them quite had what he was looking for. Then it was brought to his attention by casting director Allan Foenander that a young dancer named Emma Samuelson might be worth meeting. She was the daughter of Lighting Company owner Michael Samuelson.

Emma arrived to meet Kevin, and he knew there and then he had his Princess Zuliera. There was a problem, though. She hadn't really done anything acting-wise, and as such was not a member of Equity. The unions were powerful then, and Equity particularly so. No membership, no job. But to qualify for membership, one had to have a certain amount of experience. It's all chicken and egg time.

Kevin was convinced that he wanted Emma Samuelson. Therefore, there was only one thing to do: put a case to Equity.

The union condescended to a meeting with the director, producer and casting director and announced that they would send a representative out to Pinewood to meet with them. Well, I think everyone nearly died of shock when the representative arrived. It was none other than Kenneth Williams!

He sat and listened to Kevin and John putting their case, that they had seen so many young girls, but none were anywhere near as good as Emma.

Kenny sat taking notes and liked to play the grandiose a bit. After careful consideration he said that as Mr. Foenander was a highly distinguished casting director and that Mr. Connor and Mr. Dark had made many films employing many British actors, he would allow Miss Samuelson to become a member.

Great joy was sounded and John Dark announced that he'd laid on a buffet in the Pinewood boardroom. That pleased Kenny immensely and soon he was "one of the boys" again over tea and sandwiches, even telling everyone (in great detail) of his recent operation on his "bum."

Emma was cast. But John Dark wasn't quite happy. He said her name was too long (probably thinking about saving a few pennies when the titles were made!) and announced from now on she would be known as Emma Samms. That she was, and is indeed today too. A few years after this film, she went on to star in high rated soaps *General Hospital, Dynasty* and *The Colbys* in the U.S.

There had been a great deal of preparation on this film because, after

Alan on set with Mickey Rooney.

all, we had to do a lot of magical stuff—such as the flying carpets. I think we probably had more models, miniatures, process photography and rigs on this than any other I'd worked on. A lot of the magic came through the camera too, in the way we'd frame a particular shot. For instance, we might have a big crane-type rig under a carpet to create the illusion of it rising from the floor. All you see on the screen is the actors going up and up, whereas we were running around with all sorts of machinery whirring away on the set. So logistically, it all had to be very precise and spot on. And you must remember that they were essentially kid's films and they're the trickiest audience, as they'll pick up on any mistakes. Most of the cast and crew were parents, and I think that added to the production. They wanted to see a good family film that they could take their kids too, and I think we achieved that.

After this film, Kevin and John went their separate ways. I think John wanted to slow down a little, and he was getting a bit fed up of all the "producers" on his back from the American funders too. That just added further pressure on his shoulders, when really it wasn't needed. So half his time would be taken up with them. He was a very exuberant sort of producer—very English, with a monocle and handkerchief in his top pocket—and liked to work in his own way. Kevin meanwhile was young and hungry and keen to go on to bigger things, and maybe even try America. In fact, he was very brave and did just that. He and his wife packed up their belongings and flew to Hollywood with a couple of showreels and a few hundred pounds in their pockets. Kevin hawked himself around everywhere in a bid to get a job, and after a few weeks it was getting pretty desperate as what money they had was running out and they had just about enough to fly back to London. He had one more meeting to go regarding a UA film called *Motel Hell.* Either he'd get it, or the next flight home. Mercifully, the people involved took a shine to Kevin and his work, and offered him the job. It was certainly manna from Heaven.

From that Kevin carved out a career in Hollywood, mainly in TV films and mini-series. He went on to direct shows such as *Mistral's Daughter, North & South II, Remington Steele, Hotel, Moonlighting* and a whole load more. We keep in touch and I see him from time to time. I'll always have a tremendous soft spot for Kevin and the films we made together.

IX

The Beatles to Bond

I was next invited to join a young Welsh director on a horror film project. His name was Richard Marquand and the film was *The Legacy*. It was the first of five films that I would work on with Richard. I had hoped to do more, but he tragically died in 1987 at the age of 49, from a sudden heart attack.

The film had three writers, Jimmy Sangster, Patrick Tilley and Paul Wheeler. I think Jimmy had written the original story and the others had been brought in for rewrites.

When I say I was invited to join the production, what I failed to mention was that it was already underway. Dick Bush was the DoP and from what I can gather, he and Richard had a falling out and Dick walked off the film. A bit extreme, but then again I wasn't privy to all the facts. I took over and completed the film. I think there was only three or four weeks shooting left, but I got along so well with Richard that he asked me to do his next film with him, then the next and then the next. So, Dick's misfortune was my fortune.

It was a horror film in which Maggie Walsh (Katharine Ross), a young architect living in America, lands a job in England. When travelling through the English countryside with her friend on bicycles, she has an accident with an English lord who invites her to stay at his mansion. Other strange guests appear too, and slowly she finds out that there is a connection between her and this house, and that someone is playing a satanic game with her and the other guests.

It's all a bit creepy, but nicely done with a cast that also included, Sam Elliott, Roger Daltrey, John Standing and Charles Gray.

Richard was a very thoughtful and talented director, and he loved working with actors.

The Fab Four

I doubt there is anyone who hasn't heard of the Beatles. They're engraved in British, and indeed world, popular culture. When Richard mentioned his next project was to be *Birth of the Beatles,* I was fascinated. It was to be a biopic of their lives—well, the early days in any event. Little did I know that a few years later I'd be making a film that dealt with John Lennon's assassination.

It was a terrific film to work on and we had a talented bunch of young actors playing the fab four: Stephen MacKenna (John), Rod Culbertson (Paul), John Altman (George), Ray Ashcroft (Ringo) and Ryan Michael as Pete Best, dubbed "the fifth Beatle."

The film was a pretty accurate account of their early years, though it missed out on some of the alleged sex and drugs elements reported in newspapers and some books on the Beatles.

We shot all around Liverpool and in the Cavern Club (which I think is actually not where they started out, but a replica club nearby) and all around their haunts. Boy, did I know Liverpool by the time we'd finished!

My kids were big fans of the group when they were teenagers, and I remember coming into the house one day when one of the records were being played and, far from asking them to turn it off, I soon found myself jigging around the house in tune to it! I thought they were marvellous and so that was a great bonus when I was working on the film with lots of their music involved.

Acting

I was next asked to join an adventure project *Bear Island.* It was actually a film on which I stepped around the other side of the camera for once as I had a little part in the film. More on that in a minute.

It's a popular film on TV reruns, so I dare say quite a few of you will have seen it at one time or another. It was actually based on a novel by Alistair MacLean, which I think was a bit of a best seller (as all his were!). I think the screenwriters took a bit of artistic license as the film didn't stick particularly close to the book, but certainly from my point of view is was one of the best projects I'd worked on.

Peter Snell, the producer, had just scored a hit with *The Wicker Man* and so was keen to capitalize on that with a good adventure. He was able to secure Donald Sutherland, Richard Widmark, Christopher Lee, Venessa Redgrave, Lloyd Bridges and Barbara Parkins. Along for the ride came my old mate Arthur Wooster, looking after underwater sequences. The Second Unit was helmed by a young stuntman fast making a name for himself as an action-unit director, Vic Armstrong. Vic has recently worked on the last three Bond movies in that capacity. The boy's done well.

We were out on location in Stewart on the Alaskan border, which was pretty damn cold to say the least. The story was based in a scientific research center out there. It's a place which, once you're there, you can't leave for months, until the ice melts, so you can get a feel for how remote it is and how cut-off they all are.

A short way into the story, mysterious accidents and a murder take place. It is then the story unfolds of buried Nazi treasure. Of course, where there is treasure, there is greed, and greed has many facets—none of them too healthy! It develops in to a race against death and a rousing adventure film with snow carts zipping about and a very good psychological thriller element too.

I guess we were out there for about 16 weeks in total, and when you consider it took us two hours to get to the location from our base in the mornings and then two hours back at night, they were pretty long days too. We stayed in Juno, the capital of Alaska, in a pretty basic hotel there. It was very comfy, and the Red Dog Saloon down the road was particularly hospitable.

The "light" there was interesting. It was a high altitude (and cold) and as a result pretty clear most of the time. We used to have to keep the camera wrapped up warm, otherwise it wouldn't function. That's one of the things that is important to bear in mind, actually. It's all very well finding a great location but you have to think of the mechanics involved in shooting the film. There are certain temperatures below which equipment will not function. And of course the same can be said for humans too—hence pretty rigorous health and safety legislation nowadays. You can't expose people to dangers of too low a temperature for fear of them possibly passing out and thus causing knock-on effects down the line. We were okay—and there was a big crew—but I think it's the coldest I'd ever worked. We also had a couple of great Canadian guys with us, who were a big help.

Extra, Extra

As you can imagine, finding extras for the film wasn't that easy up there, and so some of us crew members doubled up as "non-speaking artistes." I was an Air Force officer in the background of one scene. Blink and you'll miss me!

We also had some sequences on a Russian ship which we sailed around and up into Juno Bay. It was fun to shoot on. My wife Sheila came up for a few weeks and joined us for that part of the shoot. The unit was quite considerate in that area, as us guys were away from our family for months, and so flying wives in for a few weeks kept morale high. Sheila didn't laze about, though. Amongst her many other talents, Sheila is a terrific cook and she also knows what boys away from home are like—we'd grab whatever food we could as and when we could. So Sheila said, "Right, I'm going to cook a meal." She scouted around local shops for ingredients and served up a wonderful roast lamb dinner. Just like Sundays at home! Donald Sutherland came and joined us along with a few mates of mine from the camera department. They all but cried when Sheila left us to go back home. I didn't mind so much, to be honest, as we were moving house and so I let Sheila handle it all whilst I kept clear of all the stress and arguments! I'm considerate like that.

I did buy her a lovely white fox fur hat whilst she was over, and she has it to this day.

Nose

I too have a little souvenir of that film which I carry around with me—on my nose, in fact. There was a scene with a helicopter flying in and I thought I'd try something a bit creative with my stills camera. As it came down, there was a lovely big icicle in the foreground and I thought it'd make a terrific photo. Only thing is, I'd forgotten how cold it was and as I pulled my camera away from my face, it took with it a piece of skin from the tip of my nose! So for many, many weeks there was a red round circle on the tip of my nose.

Watching

I returned home to somewhat warmer climes and wondered what might next come along. Hopefully something with a tropical location to counter the freezing cold four months in Alaska. Well, it wasn't quite tropical in downtown Iver Heath and, in particular, Pinewood Studios but a damn sight warmer than the place from which I'd just returned. It was a film called *Watcher in the Woods*. It was notable for a couple of reasons, aside from reuniting me with director John Hough. Firstly, it was to be the last of Walt Disney's British productions under a programme which started with *Rob Roy* 20-odd years earlier at Denham Studios. Secondly, it was to be one of Bette Davis' last film roles. She made a few TV movies afterwards, but nothing really deserving of her talents.

Goodness, she was a lady. A real formidable lady. She had a presence about her that I can only describe as "star quality." From tip to toe she was a total professional. Despite her advancing years, she never once messed up a line. She was never late and never demanded anything, other than total professionalism in return.

As I mentioned, Disney had embarked upon a U.K. program of family films many years earlier. Most of them were under the supervision of his British producer Hugh Attwooll. They included films such as *Three Lives of Thomasina, Kidnapped, In Search of the Castaways, Greyfriar's Bobby, Dr. Sin, Candleshoe* and many others. This was probably the darkest in terms of story, as it was quite a scary piece of filmmaking. It concerned an American family moving into a beautiful old English house in a wooded area. Strange, paranormal events occur in an interesting twist to the typical haunted house tale.

Their daughter Jan (Lynn Holly-Johnson) sees, and daughter Ellie (Kyle Richards) hears, the voice of a teenage girl who mysteriously disappeared during a total solar eclipse 30 years earlier. Together they help "rescue" her. Lots of eerie sound effects and scary visual touches add to make it a taut little thriller. Carroll Baker and David McCallum play the parents whilst the likes of Ian Bannen and Georgina Hale lent support.

I think perhaps, if there is one criticism of the film, it tried to blend horror, the supernatural and cuteness, which wasn't really typical of Disney fare and I think the American producers wrestled over what it should really be. I know it was re-edited and received two releases, though it didn't do very well on either occasion. I hear plans are afoot by John Hough to release his own cut of the film on DVD. I can't wait.

Bette Davis was really kind and great fun. I'd grown up watching her on the big screen, and now came my turn to light her for a film I was making. It's unbelievable. But I think we achieved the look required, making her slightly menacing but also capturing a certain element of beauty—and she *was* a very beautiful lady in her youth.

Ringo

Next up was a strange little film called *Caveman*. It was a United Artists film directed by a guy named Carl Gottlieb, and starred Ringo Starr, Barbara Bach and Dennis Quaid.

It was a prehistoric set film with loads of farting and funny creatures. That says a lot, I know, but perhaps a review in *The Guardian* sums it up by saying "worth half an hour of anyone's time, but unfortunately this is 97 minutes in length."

Well, that might be one review of the finished product; I've seen many others, most of them praising its humor and fun. It has a bit of a cult following, in fact. In terms of making it, as usual I very much enjoyed myself. We were out in Mexico on location, as there are some pretty bare and sparse areas in the hills which suited us perfectly as my task was to make a prehistoric land look mystical. I think I achieved it too.

The film is about daring caveman Atouk and his brave companion Lar, who are expelled from their tribes and journey through exotic lands, learning about the people and world around them.

There was one sequence when our cavemen friends had to eat and so they stole a great big dinosaur egg and rolled it along until they came to the edge of a cliff. They pushed it off the cliff and right on to a volcanic piece of rock. The egg smashed and in seconds they had a lovely big fried egg! It was hysterical. Then there was a giant mosquito, a drug-induced T-Rex and a whimpering Ice Monster. Why are dinosaurs extinct? Who invented the tire? Where does fire come from? This movie explains it all and more!

But the most outstanding feature of this film is its caveman language. They gave out flyers with the translation of all words at some cinemas, but I think it is more fun to figure it out by yourself. Besides, (almost) all the words are translated to English in one scene of the film. Some of the humor is a little juvenile, but the "caveman" language developed by Ringo Starr himself—I think he claimed once on the *The Tonight Show* that his favorite word was "zug-zug," which meant "having sex"—was great. Also an amusing scene where the cavemen who speak this language meet a caveman who speaks English and tries to teach it to them.

The director, Carl, hadn't made many films, but I think he was following Mel Brooks' trend for zany comedies. Parts were so funny. He'd started out as a writer (and actor) and he'd had some good successes, particularly with *Jaws*, and I think this was his second film. I held his hand a bit along the way, but he wasn't the sort of director who thought he knew it all and so he would talk and ask for my opinion, and the opinions of others, which lead to a great feeling on set.

The casting was interesting, wasn't it? A lot of people think of Ringo as just a drummer but he had actually been in quite a lot of films (including the Beatles three) before this, and so was also known as an actor. From a publicity point of view, his name had a bit of clout too, I guess. I think I'm right in saying, and I'm sure I'll be corrected if I'm wrong, that he and Barbara Bach first met on this film and were subsequently married.

Barbara Bach had shot to fame in 1977 in the Bond movie *The Spy Who Loved Me* which I had a hand in, during the pre-title sequence. Funnily enough, Mr. Bond was soon to enter my life again.

X

The Bond Years

My first encounter with the world of James Bond came in 1976, through my old chum John Glen. John had been around the business for years, first as an editor and then as a second unit director. He had quite a reputation as an action direction, which he proved so brilliantly in his first Bond film *On Her Majesty's Secret Service* in 1969. I digress.

I've known John for more years than we both care to remember. It was a very pleasant surprise therefore to get a call from him inviting me to work as second unit director of photography; for a big opening sequence in the, *The Spy Who Loved Me.* There'd been a bit of a gap between *The Man with the Golden Gun* and this one as the producers, Harry Saltzman and Cubby Broccoli, split and all sorts of legal wrangling was going on. Cubby returned to the series triumphant and wanted his first solo Bond to be extra-special, and with a big splash to open.

In June 1976, I flew with John to Canada and then on to Baffin Island, a massive chunk of rock in the Asgard range. It was there we met a young stunt skier named Rick Sylvester who had been approached by Eon Productions to perform a spectacular ski jump off Mount Asgard. I decided then that this young chap was either very clever or very stupid!

We did a recce, on top of the said rock, where there was a 3,000-foot sheer drop—and it *was* a sheer drop! When you're standing on white snow, surrounded by white snow and look down on white snow, it's actually very difficult to focus and get any sort of perspective. It was quite hairy. Rick seemed confident he could do it though and we each took a walk down to the precipice—secured by ropes—to look at possible camera angles. We then got back into the helicopter and flew around the range taking some footage and I think we got some of Rick throwing toilet rolls off the edge. Not terribly cinematic I know, but useful for seeing the effect of the wind.

We took the footage back to London to show Cubby, and John had the sequence budgeted at about a quarter million dollars. That was a heck of a sum of money for a few minutes of film—I'd made whole features for that! Cubby said "go ahead" and we did.

It was back to Baffin Island where we were billeted at an Eskimo settlement called Pangnirtung. It amazed me as it hardly ever got dark, it was daylight almost the whole time and you'd see kids playing out at 3 A.M. as to them it was still daytime. It was a funny little place and we were in a "hotel" which consisted of four massive cargo containers, like you see on ships, all joined together. The chap who owned and ran it was a strict German, crossed at your peril.

The other peculiarity to the area was the cloud. It hovered over the mountain virtually all day every day. Half of our battle was to be prepared to go when the cloud lifted. There was quite a lot of waiting around, and John then suggested we all camp out as the cloud was lightest during the early hours. Blimey, it was cold—we couldn't even boil a kettle, it was so cold. I think it was the second morning that we got the "go."

Rick got hold of a large piece of plywood about six feet by four feet and he stuck this right on the edge of the mountain at the end of his 50-yard slope. The idea was to hit the board and fly off the edge of the cliff. In fact, he got about 100-feet out, I would say.

"Right, Rick, we're doing it," I said. His face drained slightly and he disappeared over the top of the slope for a moment. I noticed him dropping his trousers—I'll leave you to imagine the rest!

In the film, we see Bond making his escape from Russian assassins on skis, and after a bit of a fight and few lovely stunts, he was to head straight to the edge of this perpendicular cliff and jump ... that's what Rick did. He started to fall and then jettisoned his skis, pulled his parachute (a lovely Union Jack). As it opened, the skis—which were falling slower—hit the top of the parachute. Our hearts were in our mouths, but the skis tumbled off and Rick disappeared down towards the glacier 3,000 feet below and our second chopper went down to collect him.

The real danger was that if Rick had slipped on the approach to the edge—and remember it was solid ice more than fluffy snow—he'd have been done for. It was so important he get that 100 foot clearance.

We had three cameras on the action. I was operating the one in the helicopter, whilst the other two were on terra firma. One underneath the takeoff point (operated by a local Canadian) missed everything. The other, operated by Brian Elvin on a tripod, took the up-and-down action.

The intention was that as Rick pulled his parachute, the chopper would go in and circle round and round him until he landed. When Rick dropped off the edge, my pilot (who was not a film man) dropped like a stone and my camera went up in the air. Eventually I got the camera back and managed to find Rick again after he'd dropped 1,000 feet.

Rick forlornly returned to the unit and asked, "Do I have to do it again?" John said, "No, thank you" and a look of massive jubilation crossed Rick's face. The film went off to be processed and when we saw the rushes we knew we had the shot—and that was that.

It was quite an assignment!

Bonding Again

John went on to do some second unit work on the next Bond, *Moonraker*, but I was off on other things. However, in 1980 John was asked by Cubby if he would be interested in helming the twelfth Bond film, *For Your Eyes Only*. He didn't have to ask twice. John asked for me to be his DoP and Arthur Wooster to be the second unit DoP, and I believe he had to work hard at convincing Cubby because I was really considered as a "modest budget" film maker, as my *Carry On* films so epitomized (aside from *The Spy Who Loved Me,* I hadn't really worked on any films on a par with the Bonds). I can imagine Cubby felt a little apprehensive at having a new director and two DoPs with very little "big film" experience. You can imagine how it went when Arthur called into Pinewood to meet Cubby and duly tripped over the carpet. Full credit to John though, he argued for us and Cubby said okay.

There were a few questions marks over the film, and namely over who would be playing Bond as Roger Moore had said he'd finished. John and I tested a few other would-bes, but in the end, Roger was persuaded to return.

Pre-production was tight, but it didn't really affect me too much as I would usually only come on a few weeks ahead to shoot some camera tests and maybe a little bit of other footage.

I'll forever remember my first day on *For Your Eyes Only* which was with Roger and Cassandra Harris walking in the surf on a beach in Corfu. We'd just set up and were almost ready to shoot when I felt a hand on my shoulder. It was Cubby. "Good luck, Alan" he said as he patted me on the shoulder, and I knew only too well what he meant—mess it up, and you're for it! I did finish the film, for those of you who wondered.

John came over to me one day and said, "We've been going for a week now, Alan, and it all seems to be fine, so maybe we're gonna make it!"

John's experience in and flair for action was something the filmmakers were keen to capitalize on, and we did have some truly fabulous action

Top: The pressure was on during these first scenes in *For Your Eyes Only. Bottom:* (left to right) Assistant Director Anthony Waye, Director John Glen, Executive Producer Michael G. Wilson, and Alan Hume—in conference, on location for *Octopussy*.

pieces. I'd usually look at having three cameras to capture everything going.

We had a wonderful cast. I was very fond of Topol, who was a smashing guy to have around a set. He was so professional, but had a great sense of fun and that's probably why he and Roger Moore hit it off so well. Then we had Carole Bouquet, a very beautiful young woman who drove that awful little yellow car. Unfortunately she was being manipulated by a Svengali, a French guy, and whilst I kept out of the politics, I was aware that she wasn't the production's favorite member of the cast. Lynn Holly Johnson was a terrific, and very accomplished, ice skater and I remember John having the discussion as to whether to find an ice skater who could act a bit, or an actress who could skate a bit. He got more than both with Lynn and she carried the role very confidently. Julian Glover was fun too, a fine stage and film actor who had great success in other big pictures after Bond. You couldn't have hoped for such good casting, really.

The aforementioned 2CV was such great fun, and we had a ball shooting those sequences. You'll remember that Bond's Lotus was destroyed at the beginning of the film and he, along with Melina Havelock (Bouquet), had to make their escape in the low-powered car. There were so many tight and winding roads; plus it was olive harvest time and all the nets were out on the hills. That was all thanks to stunt driver Remy Julienne, who I worked with again later—as I'll tell you.

I was pleased to see Rick Sylvester back for this picture. There wasn't any skiing. No, I lie, there was a little skiing in the film but that's not why Rick was brought in. It was actually for a very exciting mountain climbing sequence in Greece. There's a sequence in the film where Bond has to climb a near perpendicular mountain, on top of which was a monastery. Here's another little story for you too—the naughty monks were not at all keen on having James Bond around, so to disrupt filming they hung out their washing and made lots of noise. Not to be off-put, we found a way of getting the footage we needed.

Mountains

Back to Rick. He not only had to climb up this mountain, but fall off too. Well, fall some 300 feet or so before coming to a sudden halt thanks to his climbing rope. I know they were worried about a sudden jerk having so much force as to seriously injure Rick that John Richardson constructed a special rig—30 or 40 yards of track, along which a trolley would run. Sandbags were placed every few feet which would slow the truck, to which was attached the other end of Rick's rope. As he fell, the rope was pulled, the trolley moved in controlled (smooth) stages and it eased the sudden jolt at the bottom of the drop. Very clever.

Roger absolutely hates heights and cringed at the thought of having to climb part of this mountain, and I have to say I had every sympathy as I wasn't struck on it. But dear Arthur was straight in there with his camera, using some wonderful angles achieved by hanging off on ropes and leaning over edges ... but that's Arthur and his quest for perfection.

Arthur also shot some of the ski and bob sleigh sequences, not to mention some of the underwater stuff. It's a tough job but someone has to do it. I remember there being some problem with Carole Bouquet's inner ear and it meant she couldn't swim underwater. That was potentially a big problem, but John overcame it with Derek Meddings' help. They shot most of the underwater sequences with doubles and, for the close-ups, returned to Pinewood where I collaborated with John and Derek in shooting them "dry" behind a type of fish tank, with the wind machines blowing. To give the impression of slower underwater movement, I speeded the camera up three times its normal exposure rate. When it played back at the normal speed, it created the impression of underwater inertia. To complete the effect, Derek added some air bubbles onto the negative and I challenge anyone to spot the join in the finished film—you really would never know.

Q

Another person I must mention is dear old Desmond Llewelyn. He had several scenes in this one, and a lovely one as an Orthodox Priest. There was a very technical scene where *Desmond's* character had to operate a new computer system to trace an assassin by Bond's verbal description. He couldn't do it! He kept fluffing his lines and messing up the sequence of loading the computer. Now Roger used to love winding Desmond up—as he did us all—but here he spotted Desmond was struggling, and so took over the loading of the machine, leaving Q free just to talk about it.

It was sad that the other series regular, Bernard Lee, was too ill to reprise his role of M. They did bring him down to the set, but he wasn't strong enough to act and so they adjusted the script to introduce Bill Tanner, Chief of Staff deputizing for M, who was "on leave."

We took in some wonderful locations on the picture, and as well as Corfu, Greece, and the Bahamas (for the underwater sequences), we went over to Cortina to shoot some snow and ski sequences, as I've previously mentioned. Trust us, we landed just as the snow was melting!

You won't believe the number of trucks we had to-ing and fro-ing collecting snow from the higher ground to shovel around the location. Then, as we were due to complete and the script called for the snow to be melting away, down it fell from the heavens and we had to reverse the operation. Who said filmmaking was easy?

With principal photography over, I moved on to other things as my job was done, but of course John Glen still had some post-production work to complete, not least the editing with John Grover. Then in came Maurice Binder with his colorful titles and the lovely Sheena Easton to belt out the theme song—and feature in the opening titles. It was a tight schedule, but the premiere was set for summer '81 and the boys worked round the clock to deliver. It was a pretty special experience seeing the film on the big screen, and I'm very proud of my first Bond (and, indeed, my first big-picture experience). It was a great six months and John Glen was a terrific director to work for, as all the time he was editing it in his mind and knew exactly what he wanted. Imagine my delight when the phone rang the next year and John asked if I'd like to work on the next Bond with him. I didn't have to be asked twice!

Number 13

Octopussy involved a big location shoot in India. Most of the crew remembered it not for the stunning scenery, but for the dickey tummies they all ended up with—all except me, that is. I seldom ever ate any local food, unless it was the strongest curry imaginable, and stuck to the unit's British location food truck and its offerings. I only ever drank bottled water, and only cleaned my teeth with it too. You can get ill so quickly, and one by one I saw the crew go. Roger, being the suave charismatic Bond, managed to get through the shoot without any problems, but I did hear that on the plane home he was seldom out of the toilet. I digress a little, but the reason I mention my fanatical regime of only drinking bottled water is for an amusing—well, it's amusing now—reason. You see, on the initial recce to the "Floating Palace" hotel out there, the production manager asked me to bring back a bottle of water from its surrounds, as they were going to do some scenes with Roger in the submersible "crocodile" and obviously needed to check how dirty or clean it was. Quite religiously, as we were waiting to leave with all my suitcases packed, I trotted on down to the water, went down the steps and as I leaned over I went arse over head straight in! I didn't swallow any and, carrying this damn bottle of water, dashed over to the shower, took all my clothes off and had a long hot drenching. I left those clothes in a plastic bag at the hotel and wore some fresh ones out of my case. And they say location work is glamorous.

Again, we had a smashing cast. Maud Adams was beautiful and Louis Jourdan, who had been a very big star in his day, was charming and great fun to have on set. (He *was* sometimes a bit unsure of the British sense of humor and larking about on set.) Steven Berkoff as the nasty Russian, too … I admired them all as they were bloody good.

John Glen, I think, was much more comfortable with this one. It was his second time in the chair after all, but things just seemed to gel better. We had a longer prep time on this one, which obviously helped alleviate some of the pressure. I remember there was a bit of a panic on about who would play the new "M" as time was ticking on and we hadn't cast anyone. I think it was Roger who suggested his old pal Robert Brown (who had appeared in *The Spy Who Loved Me*) and everyone agreed. There was some talk about replacing Lois Maxwell as Moneypenny too if I'm not mistaken, but they wisely re-thought that one. Dear old Desmond Llewelyn was back as "Q" and had a much bigger role this time, although it was all studio-bound and he didn't get to go on location, much to his disappointment.

Potted Palms

The pre-title sequence was set in Argentina, but as it wasn't a place to think of filming at the time with the Falklands hostilities, we used RAF Northolt just up the road from Pinewood, along with fake palm trees! Not that you can tell on screen. We had some wonderful miniatures in that sequence. Where the Bede Jet is flown through the hangar at the end of the scene by Bond, it was proving tricky. The pilot, Corky Fornoff, was willing to do it for real but not with people running around everywhere. And so the shot of the jet flying into the hangar was achieved with a foreground miniature. Where you see the jet moving through the hangar, that was actually a life-size model attached to a stripped down Jaguar car, which drove it through. Then it was a combination of models and back projection for the exit and explosion. John Richardson was the man responsible and, boy, does he know his business.

I didn't do the Berlin sequence at Checkpoint Charlie, which came after the titles, that was my old mate Arthur Wooster and his second unit. He did most of the stuff with the twin brothers and all the knife-throwing stuff for the opening scenes. The twin brothers' knife-throwing skills came into use throughout the film and, finally, during the exciting end train sequences in Germany. Those sequences were actually mostly filmed in England. We used a privately owned place up near Peterborough, the Nene Valley Railway, where they have several miles of track and tunnels, perfect for a film crew as we had no timetable to contend with.

Top: Setting up the camera for *Octopussy*. *Bottom:* Alan, Director John Glen and crew on *A View to a Kill*.

There were some pretty hairy moments during that shoot and one in particular hospitalized Roger's stunt stand-in, Martin Grace, who smashed his hip and leg.

I know we planned it all out and had two or three cameras on it, with Arthur in a helicopter. The scene involved Bond climbing down onto the side of the moving train and looking through the carriage windows to try and catch the attention of Octopussy. It should have taken, I guess, a couple of miles of track to travel along and achieve the shots we needed. So, that length of track was checked for obstructions or potential tricky points and given the all-clear. Something went wrong initially, about 30 seconds into the shot, and John shouted for all to start again. The train was stopped, but didn't go back to the start of the track, so it was maybe half a mile down track. We started again, and then disaster struck. There was a post standing alongside the track, just past where the check on the line had ended, and as Martin clung to the side of the carriage, he went straight into the side of it. Mercifully, he was able to still hang on to the train. He'd done himself a lot of damage, but had he let go he would have been in a much worse state. When the train stopped, he let go. He was in hospital for a number of weeks. It didn't stop shooting for long though, and whilst that might seem uncaring and a bit harsh, it isn't. You see, stunt men are paid to do a job, a risky and sometimes dangerous job. Martin was committed to doing it, was willing to take the risk and did. Okay, it's unfortunate he had the accident but the film had to go on and there was so much else and so many other people involved too. That isn't to say Martin wasn't taken care of—Cubby saw to that. He had the best treatment and help money could buy, and before we wrapped Martin was amazingly back on set again and working.

The Other Fellow

During our production, we were all aware of a rival Bond film being made up the road at Elstree with Sean Connery. Kevin McClory, who owned the film rights to *Thunderball,* had been touting a remake for years, but in 1983 he got it all together with Connery as *Never Say Never Again.* The press did run a "battle of the Bonds" piece from time to time, but theirs seemed to be a troubled production and whilst *Octopussy* was released in the summer, they had to wait until Christmas ... and they didn't do as well as us either.

Octopussy went very well, save for the odd hiccup, and I was really getting a taste for the bigger films. I have to laugh when I think about the closing shot—everyone thought I was a genius to get it. Well, I am, but this time it was more luck than judgment. You see, the big boat with

Octopussy's girls rowing was our last sequence, and it was a daytime sequence, but by the time we were ready to shoot the sun was very low in the sky and we were fast losing light and, more to the point, the low sun was shining right up into the camera lens. In almost despair, I thought, "Oh, just shoot the bloody thing." So we did, and when I saw the result I was thrilled; it was beautiful!

One thing I always tell young aspiring cameramen is that if you've got a leading lady in a film, you have to make her look good. It's the most important thing. If she's a heavyweight star and doesn't like the way she looks, then you're out. I've never fallen foul of my leading ladies, and Maud was no exception. She was beautiful and a total joy to work with. I know both John and Roger have a particularly soft spot for her.

The other words of wisdom I dispel, whilst we're on the subject, is the importance of the schedule. It's the Holy Grail. Films are planned like a military operation and one thing I learned with the "cheap and cheerful" films I made was how to stick to a schedule and not mess around wasting time. That held me in good stead for the Bonds in particular. Take note, you aspirers.

During post-production, Cubby asked John to direct the next Bond, *A View to a Kill,* and I duly received my call, thanks to John. I was under the impression that Roger had bowed out with *Octopussy* as we seemed like going down the road of screen testing again, but then it was announced he was coming back for one more.

Silicon Chips

As I mentioned earlier, I don't really come onto films during the early pre-production period, but do get involved with recces and then various camera tests a few weeks ahead. It's also a time when I would receive a shooting script together with story boards. On the Bonds, everything is tightly story boarded, wonderfully so, by Peter Lamont's art department. We'd all sit around in meetings with the script and storyboards, and then John would quite literally pick up the storyboards and throw them away … he'd lived with them for so long, he knew them back to front and every single shot was in his head. That's very refreshing from my point of view. Yes, okay, the boards aren't thrown away and do go along to locations, but John was so prepared he'd never need them.

This time the story was set in the world of the silicon chip and, naturally enough, Silicon Valley. Oscar-winning actor Christopher Walken was signed to play Max Zorin, and I was delighted to hear that my old *Avengers* pal Patrick Macnee was also going to star as Bond's (undercover) chauffeur. The Rolls-Royce he drove was actually Cubby Broccoli's—he kept a close eye on us, and it, through production!

There was a bit of a hitch before we started as the famed "007 Stage" burned down during the shooting of *Legend*. The stage was going to house one of our biggest sets. However, Peter Lamont and his team set about rebuilding the stage, which was latter dubbed "The Albert R. Broccoli 007 Stage" and it is still in use today as the world's largest.

We went on location to Chantilly, France, and on the very first day we arrived about 7 A.M. It was very misty and as we set the camera up, John said, "Oh, look, misty and foggy. That's lovely." I thought otherwise as we had three days of shooting here, ending with the horses crossing the finishing line, and that wouldn't look too good in mist and fog. We shot it, and they did cross-cut to some of this sequence so it wasn't wasted and did look good.

The Eiffel Tower sequences proved interesting. Gaining permission to shoot anything up there is tricky at the best of times, and we wanted to jump off it—so to say. The French authorities responsible tried the production office's patience with their red tape, I know. Then we had the ludicrous situation of having permission to jump, but not having the necessary permission to land on a boat on the river.

Eventually, we got it and shot the scenes.

Arthur then started work on the taxi chase, which involved cutting a taxi in half and losing its roof. French stunt driver Remy Julienne handled the action and caused quite a stir with the locals who looked on at this crazy Renault tearing around Paris. It was over there that I first met Grace Jones. Hmmm. She was, well, a bit of a so-and-so really. To her credit she was always on time and knew her lines, but she and Roger did not get on and she did prove difficult at times. Enough said.

Off to California

San Francisco was the next big location and, boy, did we have the run of that place. That's where Cubby was so brilliant as a producer, you see, as he set everything up over there with the fire brigade, police, the City Hall (which we set fire to) and the bridges, including the Golden Gate Bridge. He had carte blanche to do what he wanted and as a thank-you Cubby had a swimming pool built for a local school (which most of the brigade's and police's children attended). To them that was just amazing, so they bent over backwards for us.

That fire engine chase was a very big and expensive sequence—all night shooting as well—and involved a lot of logistics. I never had any problems at all, as it had all been smoothed over well in advance. I learned a lot from Cubby.

The airship sequences were very exciting, and it amused me that we used a FUJI airship and on the side away from camera, it still had the big 'Fuji' logo on it. We did, of course, use a lot of models for certain shots and part of the Golden Gate Bridge was recreated (on a slightly smaller scale) on the studio lot. That's where you see Roger and Chris Walken fight it out. We used some clever back and front projection techniques, thanks to Charlie Staffell, to make it look like they were really up there. I didn't envy them "up there" as I'm not one for great heights, but John and I did take a trip up the real bridge in San Francisco, and later used it to set a camera to achieve a few of the shots you see in the film. It's certainly a long way down from the top!

The whole film was great, as were the two others before it. One thing which you don't necessarily think about when you start a Bond, is that there's a whole fan element that comes with it. It's quite something, actually. For example, I saw this chap watching the goings on on the location one day, and he stood there for ages taking a great interest. During a break, I wandered across and said I'd noticed him watching us all. He said he was very interested, but wasn't watching us; he was listening. He was totally blind. To me, that's very special—such is the popularity and magic of the Bond films. In all modesty, I still receive some fan mail all these years on. Little did I think back when I started *For Your Eyes Only*!

A View to a Kill was Roger's last Bond—and in all honesty I didn't

Happy days: on location with the Bond camera crew in India for *Octopussy*.

get the impression he wasn't going to do another one, he seemed so enthused with it all. It was my last Bond film too. I hadn't intended it to be, and I'm sure I would have done another two, the two John did with Timothy Dalton, but they were recasting. I was there with John during the screen tests—and there were quite a few, and rather famous ones too—Pierce Brosnan being one. There was going to be a ten-week gap before they needed me to start on pre-production, so I approached the production manager and asked if the company would offer me a modest retainer to hang around for ten weeks, as obviously I couldn't take another film in the meantime. I suggested maybe £200. The answer came back, pretty quickly, no.

Farewell to 007

I had actually been approached by another director to do a film, and this was partly the reason I asked for a retainer. Turning down a film is one thing when you're working on another, but to turn one down whilst you're idling around is not something I could ever suggest. However, the other production offered me £1,000 a week as a retainer in the meantime. How could I turn it down?

John Glen, who I can imagine felt a little betrayed at my departure, promoted my wonderful cameraman Alec Mills to director of photography. Alec had previously turned down *A View to a Kill* as camera operator, as he wanted to be a director of photography and was standing firm on that. I admired him for it, and was so pleased when it all worked out for him on *The Living Daylights*.

I have many fond memories of my four 007 films, and working with John Glen. I'll be forever grateful too, as it gave me my big picture break, as I mentioned, and led to more great things.

XI

In Between Bonds

Just after I'd completed *For Your Eyes Only,* Richard Marquand gave me a call to say he was about to start a film called *Eye of the Needle* and to ask if I was available. I was indeed.

It was a war story based on a novel by Ken Follett and was to star Donald Sutherland, whom I of course knew and liked immensely from our time on *Bear Island.* His co-stars were to be Christopher Cazanove, Kate Nelligan and Ian Bannen.

It was all about a World War II German super-spy, the Needle (Sutherland), who murders anyone in his way with a trusty switchblade. He discovers vital evidence about the Allied D-Day invasion plans. He makes contact with his headquarters, who tell him to head for the Scottish coast to meet up with and escape on a U-boat.

When his small boat is shipwrecked before being picked up, the Needle is washed ashore. He is saved by a young man (Cazenove) destined to never enter the war for he was crippled in a car accident a short time before and lost the use of his legs. He lives there with his young wife and child. The Needle quickly falls in love with the woman (Nelligan) who is starved of any affection or love by her husband since the accident. Soon both must decide between their love or country, and it all ends in a tense chase across the remote island.

Donald Sutherland, in my opinion, was and is a bloody good actor. In this we knew he was a Nazi spy, but we could see how he tricked people along the way and how he used them. He played that character brilliantly. There was an element of against-the-clock too as Ian Bannen played a detective hot on the heels of the Needle, so that added a great tension.

I think Richard paced it all very well. We had a lot to contend with up there too, as you can imagine how dodgy the weather is at times in the outer Hebrides, (the Isle of Mull, in fact). I think it was about an eight-week shoot up there. We weren't relying on good weather, but needed a certain amount! We did, of course, complete a lot at the studio, up at Shepperton, where Richard had greater control.

John Richardson worked on the miniatures with the U-boats and other required effects, such as the gale and storm, and Vic Armstrong popped up again looking after the stunt and action side of things.

It's certainly one of my favorite films.

I didn't work with Richard again for a year or so after completing this film, and the next one we did together was probably the biggest of my career. More on that soon.

As well as feature films, I had done a fair few television films, and my next assignment was a very big TV movie.

The Bells

It was *The Hunchback of Notre Dame.* There had been at least three, to my knowledge, earlier film adaptations but the last one had been in the 1950s with Anthony Quinn, and before that the classic RKO version with Charles Laughton.

The producer, an American named Norman Rosemont, had already made a few of the classics, or rather *re* made them: *The Man in the Iron Mask, The Count of Monte Cristo, Little Lord Fauntleroy,* etc., and so I guess the CBS-TV network in America thought that the time was right for an "event" movie and he thought it was time to look at another classic.

It was primarily a British cast and crew, and based out of Pinewood. Norman did like working with us Brits, and I'm sure we're all grateful for the work he gave us by coming over here.

Michael Tuchner was to direct. He started out as an editor at the good old BBC at the same time as Michael Apted and Stephen Frears. He went onto direct *Villain* and *Trenchcoat* and later *Wilt.* A very good director.

Anthony Hopkins played Quasimodo, Lesley-Anne Down was Esmerelda and Derek Jacobi was a particularly menacing Dom Claude Frollo.

It was all looking good to me.

Before we started, Michael ran the Laughton version in the theater for us. Boy, what a performance he gave and what a film it was. How on Earth could we equal or top it? "Destroy every print of it," offered Tony Hopkins!

Still, spurred on with our challenge, we started.

I thought Jacobi was brilliant in turning his villain into the most sympathetic character in the film. Claude Frollo has lust, whilst simmering with hate—and all the while he feels tortured and guilty. Just like Quasimodo, he is a tragic figure.

Hopkins was also outstanding. He endured hours of makeup each day. I think I'm correct in saying that he had to be up at 3:30 A.M. each day to get to the studio, have the makeup applied and be ready for 8 A.M. Layer upon layer was applied before the final touches with the false eye and eyelash, and horrible orange hair. So there he was—cauliflower ear, funny-shaped nose, horrible false teeth (with just one "fang" in the center of his mouth), a hump and club foot. Is it any wonder he opted to eat in his dressing room rather than the restaurant? Can you imagine other diners' faces?!

He looked truly terrific, though. Sadly, we didn't really get much chance to talk, as it was quite uncomfortable for him to do so, though there were certain occasions when he let his feelings be known, and I remember one in particular.

Norman Rosemont was a bit pushy as a producer and had a reputation as such. We were working on the important bell-tower sequence, I remember we had something like six set-ups and the order came through from Norman that he wanted us finished on the set that day. It was impossible. So tempers were frayed and then Tony got to hear about it, and was furious.

He insisted we all take a proper time and not rush and just see how we got on. He hated, and still hates, bullies and I think he and Norman were heading for a collision. Michael was trying the best he could to placate Norman but knew Tony was right.

Come 5 P.M. we were into the second set-up. You must remember it was a tricky sequence involving lots of stunts, and hence putting people's lives at risk. Cutting corners was not an option.

But word came through that the next day we were on another stage and were dropping the rest of these scenes. That was it!

Tony went over to see Donald, the production manager, and said that the only reason he wasn't confronting Norman was because he'd probably pull his head off. He said to Donald that unless we finished these scenes, and unless Norman stopped pressurizing the director and thus him, and stopped interfering particularly when Tony had to endure hours of make up for the scenes, then he would go on strike—or words to that effect—and to tell Norman that. The message was delivered and Norman's response was to sit there wide-mouthed.

So Tony went home adamant that he wouldn't return the next day unless a phone call was made saying that they would finish the bell-tower sequences. Well, that phone call was made and we did indeed finish our set-ups. I think Norman stayed pretty much out of the way after that, and let us get on with it ... as a good producer should when all is going to plan.

I shall skip over a little film I made with Richard Marquand for a few minutes, and devote the next chapter to it, so we're now in to 1984 and *Supergirl.*

Supergirl

Of course, you'll have all seen one of the *Superman* films with Christopher Reeve I'm sure. Well, I think it's fair to say that this film was cashing in on those films' popularity and success, though sadly it didn't quite emulate either in the event.

It was a very big project, and a great one to be involved with.

Young Kara (Helen Slater), living on Argo City, a floating spin-off of her cousin Superman's home planet, Krypton, accidentally releases the satellite's power source, the omegahedron, which heads for Earth. Impulsively, she pops into a nearby spaceship and flies after it. Once on Earth, Kara assumes the identity of Linda Lee, a brunette schoolgirl roommate of Lois Lane's sister.

Meanwhile, wicked sorceress Selena (played by Faye Dunaway) tries to acquire the magic force. She was very fussy about how she looked, and insisted on bringing in her own make up man from America. Dunaway wasn't difficult, really, as once I'd gained her confidence and—as always with my leading ladies—insured she looked good on screen, she was fine.

There was a terrific amount of blue screen and wirework and it was more of a logistical exercise than anything else. There was, of course, a dedicated team specifically to carry out and look after these sequences, but all under my supervision. Naturally it was all tightly storyboarded so we all pretty much knew where we were, what was next and so on. You might think working on a big film like this is far more complicated from my point of view. Well, that's true and then again not true. True, there is a lot more to think about, but then again I have lovely big sets to work on and am not in a cramped little stage with no room for lights. There are also many, many other people on the crew, so I have a good gang around me—all I have to do is say what I want and it's done. So what you might gain in size and complication, you find is compensated for with a bigger crew and bigger space!

On the backlot at Pinewood they constructed a wonderful Midwest town. Walking up the street I marveled at the shops and business fronts

... but that's all they were, fronts. If you peeked behind them, you'd see all the scaffolding and plywood. It was all totally false, but it looked convincing. This was the same lot where Metropolis was constructed in the *Superman* films, so there was a lovely feeling of continuity about it all, if you see what I mean.

Helen Slater was a lovely young lady. Very

Right: **Setting up for a take on** ***The Runaway Train. Bottom:*** **Helen Slater as** ***Supergirl*** **with the crew.**

professional, and very beautiful. She also did a lot of her own stunts and that was important to the production. Sure we can have doubles and stunt people, but there are times when you need a close-up that has to look convincing, and Helen was a real trouper on that front. Considering it was sometimes a little precarious (and it was her first big film, and first brush with these types of stunts), she never grumbled. It was sheer joy.

I think the idea was to have a sequel or two (much like *Superman*), but alas the film didn't do that well at the box office and plans were scrapped. I was sorry about that as I'd have liked to have done another one.

All Aboard

Runaway Train was next, and it remains another favorite of mine. It was bloody freezing too up in Alaska. Have you noticed that I tend to go for these cold climate pictures, and always end up liking them best!

Jon Voight and Eric Roberts starred. It was quite a gruesome film to be honest, and not for the faint-hearted. But it won both actors Oscar nominations, and I'm particularly proud to have had a small hand in helping them achieve that.

The director, a Russian chap named Andrei Konchalovsky, was terrific. He knew what he wanted, he didn't hang around and he kept spirits high. He had directed quite a few films in his native country, but I think this was his second English-language one. He made a few more afterwards, including *Tango and Cash* with Sylvester Stallone.

The story involves a high security prison and the breakout and subsequent escape of two highly violent (and foul-mouthed) prisoners. We actually shot inside a real high security prison, in Montana I think, and although it had been closed down for some years by the time we got there, it was a particularly creepy place. I know Andrei wanted a feel of real prison, but this was too realistic for my tastes! Still, we made good use of the location and would you believe even had "technical advice" from a couple of guys who'd served 20-odd years there for murder! Surprisingly, quite a lot of the lifers who'd secured release settled in the local community, and married local girls. Amazing, isn't it? And they were very nice guys!

Jon Voight transformed himself for this film. His physical appearance, his voice and whole demeanor. He was chillingly brilliant. I remember one scene where we're shooting into his cell, and it's pretty dark. As the camera moves in, his teeth almost light up and then his eyes, and you see real menace in them.

His character, Manny, is determined to escape the prison though he knows his chances of survival are low. But he's escaped from every other prison, and is determined to do so again. But prison warden Renken (John P. Ryan) has other ideas. He wants Manny dead and proceeds to systematically torture him ... and even ends up welding him into a solitary cell. It only serves to heighten Manny's resolve to escape.

He forms a sort of odd-couple relationship with young Buck (Roberts), who follows Manny when he makes his clever escape. They run for miles across inhospitable terrain whilst being hotly pursued by Renken. They then come across a railroad yard. It's a place where goods trains are stationed and/or stop off.

They climb aboard one of the goods wagons and lie low. What they don't realize is that there is just a skeleton staff operating everything and as the driver of the train they are on is maneuvering the engine, he suffers an accident and falls off—but the train is set in motion. What follows is, of course, the runaway train adventure. The train speeds across the Alaskan frozen lands at great speed. Well, not actually, as we undercranked the camera to about six frames per second, rather than 24. This will give the impression (when the film was run at the standard speed) of a much faster-moving train. We had to, as it wouldn't have been safe to travel at high speeds as not only did the actors (eventually) have a lot of action on this moving train, there was also us poor camera guys to consider!

The tagline was "Once it starts, nothing can stop it" and that was exactly it! This train was out of control and accelerating.

It takes a little while for our convicts to realize what is going on, and it is only after Rebecca DeMornay turns up (as the guard on the train), having jumped several carriages, trying to make her way forward to stop the train. They have no choice but to believe what she says and to try and make it forward to the engine. Several nail-biting attempts see their efforts fail. The action on board the train is quite stunning, and the suspense was terrific.

There is a scene where, in trying to make it to the engine, Manny slips and ends up in between two carriages, perilously dangling over the fast-moving ground below. That is a really tense sequence. We actually filmed it using the old-fashioned method of a rolling drum background; we were in a studio, with only perhaps a few feet between Jon and the floor, in between which we slotted in a revolving background painted on a drum. It worked brilliantly with the right lighting, camera angles and movements—and you'll believe it was all taking place for real.

I won't spoil the ending by telling you what happens, as I urge you to see this one if you haven't already.

Although it was a cruel and cold story, we managed to add nice touches of comedy and I think some of the landscapes we photographed across were beautiful. Whilst modesty usually prevails, I will also add here that many reviews did praise the "stunning photography." One industry periodical, *Sight and Sound*, actually said: "Nervy, exciting violence; immaculate, metallic camerawork; unstoppable pace."

John Lennon

I mentioned a little earlier a film I made about the Beatles. Well, it was only a couple of years after that when John Lennon was assassinated outside his New York apartment building. It was an event that shook the world.

John and Paul McCartney were probably the two most successful and prominent of the Fab Four after their split. And I guess John's relationship with Yoko Ono was much reported-on.

John & Yoko: A Love Story was the story of the two, from their first meeting through to John's untimely death. It was a TV movie, produced by Aida Young. You might recognize her name, as she was one of the two—Betty Box being the other—women producers in the U.K. through the '60s and '70s. It was predominantly a business dominated by men, but these two tough—but nice!—ladies made it to the top and made many dozens of films. Among Aida's were *She, One Million Years B.C., Scars of Dracula, Dracula Has Risen from the Grave, When Dinosaurs Ruled the Earth, The Secret Life of Ian Fleming* and many TV spin-off movies such as *Steptoe and Son, The Likely Lads* and so on.

Mark McGann played John whilst Kim Miyori played Yoko. There was a good supporting cast too, and if you watch the film carefully you'll see a young delivery boy. He was played by an unknown actor (and he was uncredited). His name? Mike Myers. He's now rather famous from playing Austin Powers of course!

We filmed a lot around London and the home counties, and then we moved on to New York and even filmed outside his apartment near Central Park where he was shot. That was quite eerie. Yoko Ono was very supportive of the film, and I recall we were all invited to have dinner with her one evening in New York. I found her to be a lovely lady, and very interesting. She was very much in love with John, and it was a great tragedy that he was murdered. He was such a talented man with so much to offer, and I doubt we'll see many like him again.

XII

Star Wars: Return of the Jedi

I doubt there are many people who haven't heard of *Star Wars*. Well, the series is continuing to this day, making millions and millions at the box office. Episode VI, as it was dubbed, was to be titled *Revenge of the Jedi* and, like the first two, was to be filmed in Britain at Elstree Studios.

After his earlier successes, Richard Marquand was asked if he would like to direct the film. I'm sure it was an offer he didn't have to even think over!

Richard called me and told me of the film, which had then changed titles to *Return of the Jedi*, and asked if I would be interested in lighting it for him. Well, it was an offer I couldn't refuse. However, George Lucas had the final say in appointments and asked to see some of my earlier work. I think we screened *For Your Eyes Only*, and on the strength of that he agreed to my being offered the DoP role on the film.

I remember George Lucas' name cropping up some years earlier when I was working on *From Beyond the Grave* with Kevin Connor. Kevin came in to the studio one morning saying he'd seen the most marvelous film the night before, *American Graffiti*, directed by George Lucas. I hadn't heard of the guy, and so thought I'd better go and see it. Well I did, but have to say it wasn't really my sort of film. That said, it was obviously a lot of other people's sort of film as I believe it cost $750,000 to make and it grossed $55 million. I don't think any of us realized that he was just getting started too, as that was a fraction of what his later films would gross.

George was very much a hands-on producer, and would always be around and have a big say in things that were going on. He was a very generous man and laid everything on that was required, including first class hotels and travel. But in return, he expected me to produce the goods!

I guess it was a bit daunting, just as doing my first Bond film as DoP was, because you knew that the *Star Wars* films that had gone prior were terrific successes and this one had a lot to live up to and had to live up to it. There was a certain amount of pressure, as there is on all films, to get it right and bring it in on time and budget—but perhaps more so on this one. I felt pretty nervous ahead of starting, but was fortunate to have a lot of friends and familiar faces on the crew with me, so it wasn't as though I was working with a gang of strangers. In fact, I confessed to the production designer Norman Reynolds that I was feeling a touch of the jitters, and he just said, "Don't worry, it's only a film, a bit bigger than your last one but just a film all the same." I suppose that helped put it in perspective for me, and instead of thinking of it as the third in the massively popular series, with millions waiting to see what we were going to do with it, I just thought, "Right, here we go again." I wasn't complacent, you understand, but needed to feel comfortable with doing it rather than terrifically nervous.

Norman had worked on the first two films, and just completed *Raiders of the Lost Ark,* and so he knew what he was talking about!

I think we were conscious, though, that *The Empire Strikes Back* was a damn good film, probably better than Episode IV, and so we had certain standards to maintain.

Elstree

We set up office at Elstree Studios in Borehamwood and it was probably one of the last big blockbuster films filmed there, along with a Bond and *Indiana Jones,* before most of the lot was sold off to Tesco in the late 1980s. That was a very sad story. The studio had been known as British International Pictures Studios, ABPC Studios (Associated British Picture Corp), EMI, EMI-MGM and Thorn-EMI (at the time we were there). A few years later, when Thorn-EMI ran into financial problems, they sold the complex to Cannon Films, who subsequently sold it to Brent Walker on the proviso a large chunk of the lot could be developed (in this case, for Tesco supermarkets). In moved the bulldozers and a great part of British filmmaking history was flattened. The much-reduced-in-size studio limped along until 1994 when Brent Walker and Hertsmere Council locked horns over the studio's future. Brent Walker had been accused of "running it into the ground" and were not investing as had been a condition of their approved take over. The studio became a ghost town and, after legal action, two years later was sold to the council by Brent Walker for £1.9 million. Slowly but surely it has been brought back to life with a £12 million investment plan and a steady stream of film and TV productions. There is a tremendous history associated with this studio, including the first talkie ever filmed (*Blackmail,* directed by Alfred Hitchcock) and great films such as *Ice Cold in Alex, Moby Dick, The Dam Busters, Look Back in Anger, Lolita, The Anniversary, Murder on the Orient Express* and, of course, *Star Wars.*

When *Empire Strikes Back* was being prepped for production, it became apparent that the stages at Elstree were not sufficient for all of the sequences, and so a new enormous silent stage was built on the backlot. That survived the bulldozers and was sold to, and erected at, Shepperton Studios in the 1990s.

Obviously, I watched the two earlier films again a couple of times to get a feel for the stories and characters, and indeed the effects and overall look Lucas was striving for. I actually remember seeing Episode IV in the cinema, on the big screen, and the opening sequence of the spaceship coming into frame drew gasps. It was cutting edge stuff.

Jedi is considered a brilliant full circle and evolution of the saga by many fans. I think they're right too.

Incidentally, when we set up production there was a terrific amount of press, media and fan interest in the film and this of course was wonderful, but it also had its downside. For instance, if we wanted to film on a particular location and we called up saying "This is the *Star Wars* office," news would spread like wildfire and we'd have hundreds of people turn up. Of course, when you're on a tight schedule and when you want to maintain secrecy (so as not to spoil the film's impact), then that isn't always particularly helpful. And so from then on we all said we were working on a film called *Blue Harvest.* It was a way of throwing a bit of sand over our tracks! Not many people knew much about this mysterious film that had gone into production, which was just as well.

I think it's fair to say that *Jedi* (as I shall now revert again) had the most creatures and monsters of the first three episodes produced. In *Empire,* reference was made to Jabba the Hutt, but you never saw him until *Jedi* (save for the late 1990s re-mastered re-releases of earlier episodes). The creation and filming of these monsters was quite a thing, and quite a challenge for the films' special effects team. They were breaking new ground with each new one, and that throws up a bit of uncertainty each time too—will they be ready in time, and when they are ready will they work?

Monsters

I remember they had two monster workshops just for this aspect of the film. One was at Industrial Light & Magic in California and the other at Thorn-EMI Studios. George Lucas invariably thought up the concepts behind the creatures and Richard Marquand provided additional guidelines to the designers. Phil Tippett was the guy at the American end of the project and I know he and Norman Reynolds were in constant touch about scenic specifications, and indeed with Richard about the characterizations. Of course, when I came onto the picture, most of this work had been completed, but I still got to see a fair bit of it going on, into the production period, and never ceased to be amazed at the creations. I know in America they built a lot of the "creature costumes" around bodies of people in the special effects department, rather than for specific actors. It was a case of finding an actor to fit the suit! Doing it the other way around would have needed a financial luxury that even we didn't have. They made a whole load of monsters in sizes ranging from small to large, so by reasoning of averages, they'd all fit someone.

Stuart Freeborn was a very experienced and talented makeup artist, and I forever remember his wonderful work on *Oliver Twist* when he made-up Alec Guinness as Fagin. Stuart was on this film and responsible for Special Creature Design and Make up. Terrific guy. I remember him telling me that a lot of his ideas actually came to him at night. He'd wake up, often only after an hour's sleep, and have an idea. He'd then rush to write it down—notes on how to make things operate, mechanics, how they move and so on.

It was a long process as I know they designed the creatures, then sculpted a likeness before mould-making, rubber-running, trimming, painting and then the final tweaking to get the look just right.

Now, there were a couple of basic ways of operating these creatures. Sometimes we'd have an actor inside a suit, like R2D2 and C3P0 for example. Or for some of the more bizarre-looking creatures, there might be an addition of a cable running up the actor's back into the mask, and that cable might control a number of facial movements, including the eyes. The cables would run along the stage floor to a nearby rig, and these rigs would be operated in strict coordination to a choreograph plan. Almost like a storyboard, you might say. They had air pipes up there too, so as when a button was pressed, air would inflate lips or cheeks or the creature would pooch out. Then there'd be puppets, of all types!

The puppets were a bit more complicated in terms, of course, of facilitating the puppeteers. So dear old Norman had to think on a couple of levels when designing the sets, as they had to both accommodate the actors and technicians—the latter out of view. Perhaps the best example of this was in Jabba's throne room. There were all sorts of creatures, and the entire set had to be built up off the floor, to accommodate puppeteers below. The entire floor was removable with individual panels like trap doors. I believe it was very expensive. Then of course you had the sheer size of crew to think about too—they all had to fit on there somewhere!

You might think that the larger the set, the more difficult it is to light too, as I touched on with *Supergirl.* The majority of sets were large ones on *Jedi* so I had lots of space to move around and hide lights in the gantries and behind parts of the set. It made my life easier on this occasion.

I know Richard spoke, in interviews, of wanting to create real relationships and real action stemming from real emotions, and while he was doing that he had some pretty challenging camera set-ups and special effects to think about too.

As to a bit of the story, following on from *The Empire Strikes Back,* Luke Skywalker (Mark Hamill) follows his Rebel Alliance friends to Tatooine, his home planet, to rescue Han Solo (Harrison Ford), the space pirate turned rebel hero who was captured by Jabba the Hutt for overdue debts.

Skywalker seems a changed man since leaving Tatooine with 'Obi-Wan' Kenobi (Alec Guinness) to fight the evil Empire. Above all else, he yearns for another chance to confront the evil Darth Vader, despite a cleverly instilled dilemma as to (whether he will destroy him or eventually turn to the Dark Side and join Vader), which runs throughout the film.

The scenes on Tatooine were very impressive. I remember Jabba's lair, the floating palace and the "almighty Sarlac" creature that lives in the sand as being particularly good.

With Lea and Solo, Skywalker and the Rebels set out to destroy an all-new Death Star that nears completion. This time the Emperor himself is overseeing the final stages of construction. The Empire intends to crush the Rebellion once and for all, while the Emperor himself schemes to bring the now powerful Skywalker to his side to work alongside (or is that replace?) Darth Vader. It was pretty much Luke Skywalker's picture, actually.

There was a great pace to it too. I recall Mark Hamill saying that it was similar to the "smash and grab" technique of the first one. We didn't hang around (did I ever?) and there was a terrific energy and momentum. We'd look at a scene and if we couldn't get it after a couple of takes, we wouldn't get hung up on it, we'd move on. I believe the pace on *Empire* was more leisurely. In fact, I'm not telling tales out of school, but they did have a lot of technical problems and in the end it went six weeks over schedule. I think George was adamant it wasn't going to happen again! Just like the first film, it was go, go, go. Mind you, that first film ended up with a budget of just under $10 million. *Jedi* was budgeted at $32.5 million (and on schedule).

Bikes

There was certainly a bit more action in *Jedi* and a lot more effects. The great bike chase through the forest was quite a complicated little sequence, though quite simplistic. We had all the actors on a blue-screen stage on the machines, and meanwhile had sent out a camera team to shoot the background plates. Basically, they took a steadi-camera and walked through the forest, shooting as they walked at about one frame per second. So when the film was processed and played, it looked like they were moving very fast. Into this we added our actors.

It was all tightly storyboarded of course, but not so much as to restrict us if we needed to do something extra or different.

George never interfered either, nor was he ever critical. That was always my fear—no, that's wrong, it wasn't a fear, it was perhaps a *concern*—that George wouldn't let Richard do it all his way. But all credit to George, he did. He would always be on hand to offer advice or input, but would never force an issue.

Lucas

I didn't have a terrific amount to do with him, to be honest. I think I only ever crossed swords with him, so to say, on one occasion and that was when we were out in the Uhma desert. Richard and George were walking around looking for a set-up to shoot. My son Simon was a young focus puller on the picture, and so he was walking behind them carrying this big camera. It was pretty damn hot out there, and the camera is a heavy piece of equipment. I called out to Simon to put the camera down and wait until they found the set-up. George heard me say this and shouted over, "What's that, Alan, why did you say that?"

I just looked at him, silently. I should have said, "It's over 90 degrees and I told him to put the bloody camera down until you're ready for it." I didn't, but should have!

The sand did cause us a few delays. When the wind picked up, it could be quite nasty, so on a few occasions we had to stop shooting and take cover.

I think of the three directors (*Star Wars*, *Empire* and *Jedi*), Mark seemed most comfortable with Richard Marquand. Richard, you see, had been an actor and so he brought that insight with him.

That showed in the final encounter between Skywalker and Vader. It was a fast-moving sequence, with light sabers to kick off, and then more psychological with the Emperor pitting son against father, good against evil. It was quite a showdown and very emotional.

Guinness

I think my overall input to *Jedi* lasted about 16 weeks or thereabouts. It was a great experience and they were all great guys, the actors and crew, but if you asked me for an outstanding moment of the film I'd have to say working with Sir Alec Guinness. He was amazing. I had worked with him many, many years earlier on *Oliver Twist* but he had matured into an iconic figure within the British film industry, and one of tremendous talent. He had the most marvelous presence when he walked on the set. It was like God walking in.

He was terrific. So kind, funny and good-humored. I believe his part was filmed in a day. Certainly no more than two. I think it's fair to say that he made more money from the *Star Wars* films that in the whole of the rest of his career put together, yet in later life he hated the mass attention the films' success brought him. I guess it was a lot of modesty with a touch of disbelief. When asked for autographs by ardent fans, he'd often quip, "Get a life."

But then the *Star Wars* films were more than just films. They were people's childhoods, their dreams, their escapism. Just look at the merchandising side of it all too. It amazes me. I think George made more from licensing merchandising rights than any other film before (or since) and really changed the way films were marketed and promoted.

New Technology

I guess I was quite aware during production of George's desire to move more of the processes towards new technology and new advances. He wanted to go bigger and better and get away from some of the old (and time-consuming) techniques employed in special effects. Even back then he spoke of digital technology and how one day film itself would be replaced. And you can see how far he has come in 20 years, hav-

Alan supervises a lighting set-up for *Return of the Jedi.*

ing shot *Attack of the Clones* purely on digital. I think George is only just starting too—he has a lot more to offer us yet!

Some people ask if I was aware of how future episodes might turn out. Not really, but I do know that George had it all planned out in his head. On occasions some of the actors might ask him a question about their character—perhaps about something in childhood, like Mark for instance when he asked how Luke's parents died—and George had the answers. Episode III is due out soon, and I think that'll tie up a lot of loose ends and answer a lot of questions. As to whether he will film Episodes VII through IX, I do not know. He says he's pretty exhausted now, and I guess he would be, as long after the likes of me leaves a film, there can be a year or more of post-production, as indeed there was on *Jedi*.

I'll always be grateful for the opportunity of lighting *Jedi*, and it was certainly the biggest film I've ever worked on.

XIII

Sherlock and *Wanda*

I've already mentioned the Cannon Group and their acquisition and subsequent sale of Elstree Studios (and incidentally ABC Cinemas too). Well, that was in the late 1980s and meanwhile, a few years earlier—where we are now—they were still building their production empire.

It was 1985, in fact, and a film called *Lifeforce*. It had one of the biggest art departments, special effects crews and stunt teams on any movie I'd made. It had a sizable budget, too, at $22.5 million, and it was a rather good sci-fi film.

Tobe Hooper was the director, fresh from success with *Salem's Lot* and *Poltergeist* (he liked horror, I think)—and he was quite mad! Everything he wore was black.

He'd arrive at the café across the road from the studio every morning at 7 A.M. and would have his breakfast there and wait until 8 A.M. to walk across to the set. I got into the habit of meeting him there and we'd have a chat. We shot up at Elstree Studios, by the way, and it was essentially a vampires-in-space film. Well, it was based on a book called *The Space Vampires:* a detective story that begins when Halley's Comet returns to the solar system and the English-American team aboard the shuttle *Churchill*, making a close-up survey of the comet, discovers an alien spacecraft in the head of it.

Inside this spacecraft are some large bat-like creatures and three cocoons in which there are "dead" humans—two men and a woman. The *Churchill* takes the humans and a creature back to Earth. There the bosses of the project are amazed to find the shuttle burned out and all bar one of the crew—Carlsen (Steve Railsback)—dead. The humans from the spacecraft suddenly awake and all those who come into contact with them are drained of their "lifeforce" and in time all the victims—including most of the population of London—are turned into zombies all preying on the horrified survivors for their "lifeforce." It's up to Carlsen and Major Caine (Peter Firth) of the SAS to stop them before the whole world turns into a big blood-hunt.

It was very bloody and quite horrific and certainly not a cheery sort of film.

There were masses of make up people on the film too, creating these horrific-looking people running about.

We shot the picture in what was called "Duntonvision" and that was a type of 'scope invented by camera renter Joe Dunton. Instead of pulling the film down five perths, we only pulled it down two, and used little slots so each 1,000-feet roll of film became 2,000-feet of film—it was a cheap way of saving film!

Gerry Thomas

The Second Victory was next, produced and directed by my old friend Gerald Thomas. It was a story based on Morris West's novel and set in Austria after World War II, involving British occupation forces and the unrest following the murder of a sergeant there.

I know Australian money was involved, and we shot in Saltsburg on some excellent locations.

We had to recreate an avalanche for one sequence, and the Austrian production manager was talking it over with his team. They looked a bit puzzled. Anyway, I went over to talk to him about how we were going to shoot the avalanche and he looked at me and said, "In the tunnel over there," and he pointed to a road tunnel where a lot of our vehicles and equipment were parked. I couldn't understand what he meant, and he went on, "At about one o'clock, we have a lunch."

"No!" said I, "not 'have a lunch,' *avalanche!*"

Oh dear. Anyway, we got there in the end.

This was quite a departure for Gerald, as a matter of fact. For the past, I don't know, 30 years I guess, he'd been categorized as a comedy director. A very good one he was, but before the comedies and the *Carry Ons* Gerald directed a lot of other films, including thrillers, and secretly I think he yearned to prove he could do it again. He revelled in the opportunity. It was also a marked difference in that Gerald shot mainly on location, with only a little studio work. It was usually the other way around, and I know we had a longer schedule than ever, as it was quite a complicated story. It was probably double the length of a *Carry On* schedule!

We had a good cast too, in Anthony Andrews, Helmut Griem and

Max von Sydow, but alas the film has never been shown in Britain. Isn't that a shame?

Bob Dylan

I next received a call from Richard Marquand asking if I'd work with him on a film called *Hearts of Fire*. It was my fifth film with him, and sadly my last as shortly after completing it, he died. I wouldn't say it was his best film, it wasn't, but it was still a very interesting one.

Bob Dylan was the star, and he was pretty good actually as a reclusive pop star—and the original music was provided by John Barry. But I found Bob to be very reclusive and withdrawn. When we were shooting (other) artists' tests, he came along to watch but stood in the far corner of the stage. Perhaps he was deep in thought and contemplating his own performance, but he showed little interest or enthusiasm and I found that a bit strange, to be honest.

The female lead was Fiona, the American singer known only by her Christian name. In the film, she teamed up with Billy Parker (Dylan) for a London gig, then got spotted by a British pop singer (Rupert Everett). She and the pop singer subsequently become lovers, whilst Parker returns home to America. I suppose it's a moralistic story in many ways.

It's a shame that this was Richard Marquand's last film, as he deserved to go out with a better one. In fact, it was probably his weakest film if I'm being honest. A great shame, and I miss him very much.

Woolworth's

Poor Little Rich Girl: The Barbara Hutton Story was an American mini-series with an impressive cast: Farrah Fawcett, Burl Ives, Brenda Blethyn, Nigel LeVaillant, Miriam Margolyes, Zoe Wanamaker and many others. It was a sprawling four-hour biopic all about Barbara Hutton, heiress to the immense Woolworth store fortune. She was married eight times, and Cary Grant was one of her husbands. He was the only one to renounce all claims to her fortune, yet the couple were called "Cash and Cary." Hutton's life took her to exotic locales like Denmark and Morocco. Nearly all of her husbands treated her poorly. A social butterfly, she was a bad mother to her only son whose death in a plane crash broke her heart.

It was directed by Charles Jarrott who, like a lot of the supporting cast, was a Brit. Needless to say we got along very well, and it was terrific to travel around the world in Barbara's footsteps: Germany, Denmark and Morocco. Ultimately, it was more of a tragedy than love story, and I guess it prompts that old adage that money can't buy happiness.

Michael Caine

After a few quite serious films, I was delighted to be offered a comedy next. *Without a Clue* (or as it was called during production, *Sherlock and Me*) starred Michael Caine and Ben Kingsley. I guess you would call it a parody of the Holmes films, and blimey, there'd been an ocean of them. I grew up watching the wonderful Basil Rathbone—Nigel Bruce adventures, and have to admit they were probably the quintessential Holmes and Watson on the big screen. Jeremy Brett later made the role his own on the small screen in the 1980s, and in between scores of actors turned their hand to the character—including Roger Moore, Charlton Heston, Christopher Plummer, Peter Cushing, Tom Baker and Ian Richardson.

There had been a few comic parodies too—Gene Wilder in *The Adventure of Sherlock Holmes' Smarter Brother* and Billy Wilder's *The Private Life of Sherlock Holmes*. Ours was a good script, well-rounded, and the two leads worked well together.

It was all about how Dr. Watson (Kingsley) had hired a drunk and failed actor, Reginald Kincaid (Caine), and paid him for many years to "play" his creation, consulting detective Sherlock Holmes. However, after becoming tired of Holmes taking the credit for solving crimes (which he alone had done), an argument ensues, resulting in Watson firing the actor. Watson soon realizes that people believe Holmes to be the genius of the pair, and his own attempts to promote himself as "the Crime Doctor" fail miserably.

He has no option but to hire Kincaid again when the Chancellor of the Exchequer calls at 221B Baker Street to try and employ Holmes following the theft of the Bank of England's template for the £5 note. It turns out that the dastardly perpetrator of the crime is none other than Professor Moriarty (Paul Freeman).

In a twist at the end of the film, Holmes announces his retirement and that Dr. Watson will be taking over from him … but Watson sees the value in his creation and persuades the actor to stay on.

Thom Eberhardt was the director, having only made three other films. The producer Marc Stirdivant had been Disney's youngest ever staff producer. This picture, though, was produced by the ITC Group, and was aptly described as being "*The Odd Couple,* Victorian style."

It was a $10 million budget and an eight-week shoot. We went on location to Lake Windermere and Derwent Water, then on to Gloucester, Blenheim Palace, Syon Park and London locations, with studio work at both Pinewood and Shepperton.

Female beauty was added by Lysette Anthony. Jeffrey Jones played the infamous Inspector Lestrade.

We had a great time, and I found Ben Kingsley to be a wonderful, wonderful actor. I don't think he'd played much comedy before then, but had a great comic ability. Michael Caine had just won the Oscar for *Hannah and Her Sisters* and so was riding on a high. It all combined for a well-crafted and enjoyable film. I think it performed reasonably well too, and the reviews were pretty okay on the whole. *Variety* said of it, "This novel approach generates a few laughs and smiles, but of a markedly mild nature and with most of them provoked by the shrewdly judged antics of the two stars."

Wonderful Wanda

A film which fared infinitely better with reviews and box office was, of course, *A Fish Called Wanda*. It rates as one of the best, one of the most enjoyable and one of the most successful British films ever made.

It all came about after John Cleese had made a film for Thorn–EMI called *Clockwise*. It was a delightful little comedy set in a school where John was the time-obsessed headmaster, Mr. Stimpson. A simple trip to Norwich, to attend a headmaster's convention, turns into one of the most complicated and unbelievable journeys possible. Not to mention an absolute nightmare.

It was a good script by Michael Frayn, solid direction by Christopher Morahan and a lovely supporting cast headed by Alison Steadman, Penelope Wilton and Joan Hickson—the latter of whom played one of the three "dotty old ladies" who ensured great comic mileage throughout.

I think I'm correct in saying that this was John's first film as a leading man. He'd starred in many other films, but usually as part of a team (Monty Python) or in guest roles (such as *Time Bandits*) but had never carried a film on his own name. So this was quite a big deal for John.

It was a well-done crafted film, and one John was proud of; and as such he took an active involvement in the promotion of the project.

It performed well in the U.K., and moderately in other territories. But when it came time to release the film in America, John was very upset when told that not one single cinema in Chicago would take it. He honestly couldn't believe it, and this really stuck in his throat. The overall U.S. response was lackluster, but that only served to fuel John's resolve that he would make a film that they would book in Chicago, and furthermore that would do well there.

He sat down and started working out ideas. He'd always been fascinated by the way Americans viewed the English, and thought that would be an interesting element. One of the things he discovered was that there was a real fascination of the British justice system in the USA—particularly Crown Court. Those "silly" wigs worn by barristers, the pomposity of proceedings and so on. That was a good start. There was to be no political slant to the story, nor any hidden meanings or subtext. It was to be a straightforward comedy-drama.

A master stoke (in my opinion at least) was when John recruited his old friend Charles Crichton to work with him on the story. Charlie was one of the old-school, and brilliant with it. He started off in the editing rooms on *Sanders of the River* and *Elephant Boy* and then on the classic Ealing Comedies, soon progressing to directing them. Wonderful films such as *Hue & Cry, The Lavender Hill Mob, The Titfield Thunderbolt* and *Battle of the Sexes* ensued. After Ealing closed down production, Charlie turned his attention to TV drama. He directed many episodic shows such as *Man in a Suitcase, Strange Report, The Professionals, The Return of the Saint* and so on. He also worked with John Cleese at his company Video Arts, where they made many scores of training films. It was here that John and Charlie struck up a solid friendship. John invited Charlie to work with him on his new comedy story, with a view to directing it.

John was great with actors and dialogue, and Charlie was brilliant with the technical aspect of things, so they made a formidable team. Charlie also drove the story and never lost sight of the purpose in a scene. A lot of directors overlook that and often get caught up in their own indulgences. Charlie never did.

Once it began coming together, John fixed a meeting with Alan Ladd, Jr., at MGM in Los Angeles. Not everyone could have done this, but John had a certain profile and fame which, I guess, he could use to his advantage from time to time. The response was enthusiastic.

A year or so after *Clockwise,* John had made a film called *Silverado* in which Kevin Kline was one of the co-stars. They had hit it off immediately, and I think Kevin had grown up on Monty Python humor, and so they were well-suited.

He'd also recently seen a film with Jamie Lee Curtis, and was fascinated and captivated by her.

He decided that the "American" element in the film would be brilliantly played by these two actors. And so he and Charlie began tailoring the characters with them in mind.

The fourth major character came in the shape of Michael Palin, longtime collaborator and friend from the Monty Python days.

John and Charlie worked for months on end, developing the characters and the storyline and bit by bit, touch by touch, it all began coming together.

The storyline was simple, yet ingenious. A jewel robbery in London's diamond district of Hatton Gardens goes swiftly and smoothly. The diamonds are stashed and the gang separate. But double-crossing follows! Kevin's character, Otto, was a psychology-quoting heavy with a fierce temper and hatred of being called "stupid;" Jamie Lee was the beautiful Wanda (who is secretly double-crossing the other gang members with Otto); and Michael Palin played environmentalist and animal lover Ken. The fourth gang member, George (Tom Georgeson), the brains behind the robbery, ends up in prison after being the subject of a police tip-off. He and Ken suspect Otto is behind it all. But what they didn't bank on was George moving the diamonds somewhere else.

Wanda thinks the only way to find out where is by getting close to George's barrister, Archie Leach (John Cleese). "Archie Leach," by the way, was Cary Grant's real name.

The script was sharp and the characterizations funny and well-rounded. Incidentally, Jamie Lee Curtis was actually a bit unsure at first about playing comedy. She didn't think she was funny, but in rehearsing (John was a relentless rehearser) she found that it was funny, and she was funny. Thereafter, she played it brilliantly, with cheeky grins and looks in all the right places.

The only witness to the robbery is an aging lady (Patricia Hayes) with a love for her three pet Yorkshire Terriers. George tells Ken that she must be killed (much to Otto's delight). Ken brings in a killer Doberman to do just that, and they sit in the back of a van, waiting for the old lady to emerge with her dogs.

The Doberman in question was quite a nice dog, in fact, and not particularly vicious (we used a second dog for the closeups of snarling teeth). Its temper was aroused by firing a harmless burst of air onto its testicles. Well, wouldn't you jump?! Rather than killing the old lady, however, the Doberman picks up and runs off with one of the three Yorkshire Terriers.

Another failed attempt follows, and sees the second of her three dogs killed. The third attempt in this wonderful comic masterpiece of a subplot sees her third dog flattened by a piano which was being hoisted to an upstairs apartment. The shock of which kills the old lady! Mission accomplished.

It was a brilliant bit of writing, actually, to have an animal lover trying to kill an old lady but instead, one by one, killing her dogs by accident.

When the piano fell on the last dog, we had a dummy made—a

"flattened" dog—which we placed on the road for the pick-up shot. Now, there was a bit of debate about this. Props had come up with some squeegee-looking entrails where were laid beside the dog, to suggest its guts had been squashed out. John thought it would add comedy. There was uncertainty though, and the producer Michael Shamberg suggested we do a shot of the dog without the entrails, for safety. When the first cut was shown to Alan Ladd, Jr., he was adamant that the entrails should be removed as, far from finding it funny, he felt sick. John heard his argument and readily agreed to insert our "safety" shot without the guts. Ladd was absolutely right. Test-screening the latter take produced great laughter, as it was cartoon-ish in style, whereas the realistic guts left everyone quiet.

Similarly, there was a sequence where Otto used cat's tails for target practice. We had a few cats (with tails erect) walking by, and he fired off the tips of their tails. It was all done in a very humorous way, but when the film had to be shortened at the end of production, this bit was cut. I think the balance of "animal cruelty" was being tipped a little too far, and so the removal of this scene helped trim the running time and tilt the balance back too.

Another memorable scene is the one where Leach and Wanda nip off to a river side flat near Tower Bridge to "consummate" their passion (and for her to get the information she wants). Unbeknownst to them, Otto has followed to ensure Wanda doesn't go too far. But Otto is eventually spotted, or at least is in earshot when Archie describes him as "stupid."

The next shot is of Archie Leach apologizing. The camera pulls back and we actually see he is suspended upside down from a fifth floor window by Otto, who is demanding an apology. It's hilarious.

Of course, to create the desired comic effect, it was obvious that John would have to physically do this himself. He must have been mad!

We rigged a safety belt on him with strong wires fed down his trouser legs to both support him and offer the necessary safety should anything have happened. On the floor below, we set up a platform that could be slid out with John flat on his back. He was lying below the window he was to dangle from, and thereby could inch his feet up into the air so as when the platform was pulled back in, he was literally hanging by his feet out of the window—full of apologies to Otto.

It was a great sequence and I remember Charlie saying it was the best piece of upside-down acting he had ever seen!

I mentioned earlier how Jamie didn't feel she was funny, but trusted John and took his direction and rehearsed it until she saw she was indeed very funny. Well, the tables turned here a bit. In the "love" sequence, Jamie insisted that they not rehearse, but play it to capture a spontaneity. John was unsure. He never saw himself as a "romantic lead" and was very uncomfortable and stiff (so to say)—but Jamie argued that was perfect for the character. Jamie was absolutely right.

Many lovely sequences followed, and then we came to the climax at Heathrow airport. The idea was that Archie and Ken were pursuing Wanda (who now had the diamonds), who was being pursued by Otto ... a chase sequence, you might say. It all ends up on a building site at the airport with wet cement and steam rollers.

Otto gets stuck in wet cement and can't move his feet. Ken jumps on to a great big steam roller determined to flatten the brash American whom he hates so much—albeit at two miles per hour. He does, though! But the bit you don't see is where we cut away the central segment of the roller so that Otto could just stay put and let it move over him, and it looked (from the side) like he was being flattened. I remember in initial test screenings, there was uproar about Otto being killed off. And so we re-shot the ending to have him appear at the plane window when it takes off (with Wanda and Archie—who are now genuinely in love) on board.

The steam roller, incidentally, was a particularly large one. The front roller must have been six feet high and that was purposely written in by John. He wanted to see this great thing at eye level coming towards Kevin. It really added to the comic effect.

The cast and crew of a *A Fish Called Wanda* on location near Tower Bridge, London.

It was a truly, truly wonderful film.

Kevin Kline won the Oscar for Best Supporting Actor, John won the BAFTA for Best Actor, and Michael for Supporting; and Charlie was nominated for his first Oscar. I wish he'd have won it as it would have been so brilliant for him, at 77 and on his last film, to have achieved that. But he did achieve terrific box office success! And I'll let you in to a secret here. On *Wanda* John gave me a tiny percentage of profits which, in fact, turned out to be worth a pretty decent sum of money.

After *Wanda,* John kept in touch with me, and then in the early 1990s he announced that he was working on a follow-up script. He wrote to me saying that it was coming along and he wanted me on the film, and to be ready and so on.

In 1995 I think it was news came through that *Death Fish II* was going into production with Robert Young directing. I'm not quite sure what went on, but I was never offered the film. I suppose the director wanted his own DoP? I must admit to being very upset actually, as I was very much looking forward to working with the gang again. I wasn't offered any reason as to why I wasn't asked. The film was all set in a zoo, which they recreated at Pinewood, and it was a very big picture. But I don't think they had the script sorted out well enough, as after editing and re-editing the test screening feedback came in, saying that there were a few problems and the main one was Kevin Kline's character was killed off too soon.

Meanwhile, all the actors had gone on to other projects and Michael Palin had gone off around the world on one of his TV travel documentaries. So it was a year later that they came back for (expensive!) re-shoots, with a new director, Fred Schepisi. I hear that upwards of 70 percent of the story was reworked and re-shot. That's a hell of a lot. Consequently the budget must have doubled. Sadly, it didn't emulate the success of *Wanda.* I was genuinely sorry too.

XIV

Jack and Shirley

I hadn't long worked with Michael Caine on *Without a Clue* when I was offered his next project: *Jack the Ripper*. Like Sherlock Holmes, there have been many films made about the Victorian murderer, and a great many actors have portrayed him. This was, perhaps, the definitive TV mini-series. It was, significantly, Michael's first mini-series and the first British show to air in prime-time (on CBS) in the USA. Michael had not long returned to the U.K. after being a tax exile in the U.S.A. for many years, and undoubtedly his casting was paramount in CBS backing the project in collaboration with Euston Films of London.

It was directed, co-written and produced by David Wickes, who had made a name for himself directing TV shows and movies such as *Sweeney!* (1976) and *Silver Dream Racer* (1980). It was said the screenplay was partly based on new information from previously unreleased Home Office files. Such was the hoopla surrounding the unveiling of the real Ripper that David announced he would film several endings to the show and only on the night of transmission would we discover which one was true.

"For over 100 years, the murders in Whitechapel committed by Jack the Ripper have baffled the world.... What you are about to see is a dramatisation of those events. Our story is based on extensive research, including a review of official files by special permission of the Home Office and interviews with leading criminologists and Scotland Yard officials...."

So went the opening narration from the show.

Michael was perfect as Chief Inspector Frederick Abberline,—a straight-talking Cockney police officer, and Lewis Collins was solidly cast as his assistant Sergeant George Godley.

As usual, the schedule was very tight and we had something like 60 sets on the production, so you can see it was quite an epic. Victorian London was recreated at a disused asylum in Virginia Water, Surrey, which was a very eerie place to work. It seemed untouched since closure, with beds there and even operating theaters. It gave me the shivers. I was far happier on location at Greenwich Naval College and over at Pinewood.

People sometimes ask if period costumes and settings cause more problems. The answer is no; in fact it's easier and more creative. In our case, the sets and costumes were there already, we added the odd horse and cart and bit of smog to complete the effect. It can offer up some wonderful lighting opportunities!

At Pinewood around this time, Dan Curtis was shooting *War and Remembrance,* quite a big project. For some reason he seemed quite cold towards us and David Wickes and we couldn't quite figure out why. All was revealed when David confronted him about it a few weeks into the shoot. You see, our female lead was Jane Seymour and he wanted to cast her in his show, but was told that she'd only be available four or five weeks after his start date because she was making our film. Dan was resentful of that, but I think it all got ironed out!

So who was the Ripper, you ask? I'm not telling—you'll have to watch the show!

Incidentally, it was number one in the U.S. ratings and had the distinction of being the first U.K.–produced mini-series to be so, and in the U.K. it even toppled firm ratings winner *Coronation Street* for the top spot.

Tony Hopkins

My second film with Anthony Hopkins was a great dramatic one. It was called *The Tenth Man* and was based on a World War II story by Graham Greene. It reunited us with producer Norman Rosemont (from *Hunchback*) and all signs of past tensions and disagreements had long been eradicated.

Greene wrote the story during his time as a contract writer for MGM. He described it as being a two-page idea about the liberation of France in 1944. Some 40 years later, these pages (some 60,000 words in fact) were discovered in a Hollywood vault by an MGM archivist, and subsequently published in book form in 1985.

Anthony Hopkins played a French lawyer, Jean Louis Chavel, is imprisoned by the Germans during the occupation in 1941. One day a Nazi officer comes into the cell and tells the inmates that three men are going to be executed (they are about 30 men in the cell). Just for fun, the Nazi officer says that they themselves will have the "honor" to choose which three of them will die. They decide to draw lots.

They mark three of the lots with an X and draw. Chavel gets the last X. He panics and offers all his material possessions, including his house and money, to anyone who is willing to die in his place. A man dying from lung cancer accepts. He is going to die anyway and he wants the money and the house for his poor sister and mother. However, when the day of execution comes, Chavel suddenly regrets everything, but it is too late.

At the end of the war, Chavel, posing as one of the other prisoners, returns to his home, which is now occupied by the executed prisoner's sister, Therese, who bitterly awaits the return of the man who had indirectly caused the death of her brother. His real identity is unknown to Therese. "Chavel" is meanwhile invited to stay as a caretaker—as she takes pity on her dead brother's prisoner friend—and he is to identify the man who traded places with her brother, should he return to the house. The relationship between "Chavel" and Therese develops until, one night, someone calling himself Chavel turns up at their doorstep.

We filmed extensively in an old chateau in France, and my old friend Jack Gold was the director. We had last worked together on *The Bofors Gun*. It was nice to be in France again too; I had worked there a few times before, particularly on my last Bond film, and found it a lovely place to work. It's all very relaxed and easygoing! Mind you, having said that, we filmed the whole piece in 24 days in August, and had a very quick turnaround as it aired on American television on December 4, 1988.

Shirley

Now then, what came next? Oh yes, dear Shirley. Well, there are two very special Shirleys in my life. The first is Shirley Bassey as she married my brother Kenneth, and we became great friends. I know my wife Sheila got on very well with Shirley and their daughter, who so tragically died in 1985. I'm afraid it was a rocky road with Kenneth. He produced, directed and wrote films and documentaries, mainly music-orientated, in the '50s and '60s and that's how he met Shirley. They married soon afterwards, but there was a lot going on in Kenneth's life that made it difficult for him and Shirley; it sadly ended when he committed suicide in 1967.

However, we keep in touch with Shirley and usually hear about what's going on in her Christmas card to us. We'll always be very fond of her.

The other Shirley in my life is *Shirley Valentine*. She's quite a lady too. It was playwright Willy Russell who dreamed up the story of the bored and formidable Liverpool housewife for the stage. It worked so well that long West End runs followed along with touring versions. It still tours to this day, and somewhere in the world you can bet your bottom dollar that there is a stage playing host to the play every day.

Such was the success of the play that producer John Dark came out of his retirement in Spain. Well, no, that's not true, he hadn't really retired, but after *Arabian Adventure* he took a lot of time out, and made only one other film, the Thorn-EMI–produced flop *Slayground*. John and Lewis Gilbert were very keen to transfer the story to the big screen. I'd met Lewis during my tiny stint on *The Spy Who Loved Me* but of course knew John Dark of old. It was John who offered me the job, and how delighted I was to accept.

Lewis was a lovely man who shared my childish sense of humor. He was also a very good actor's director and, in particular, very good with women—well, I mean in the director-actor sense! After all, you only have to look at *Educating Rita* and the performance he extracted from the wonderful Julie Walters. Lewis is of the "old school" and I knew as soon as he stepped onto the stage floor that he had it all worked out in his head.

Pauline Collins had won plaudits in the West End and Broadway productions, and both John and Lewis were keen to cast her in the film lead. It was a tough battle, though, as Pauline hadn't made a film as a leading actor before and the casting director, Allan Foenander, was continually receiving suggestions of American actresses from the U.S. studio backing the film. But ultimately Pauline was cast as Shirley Valentine-Bradshaw. The rest of the cast came together: Tom Conti was excellent as the Greek would-be seducer Costas Caldes; Bernard Hill was her down-putting husband Joe Bradshaw; and an inspired piece of casting came with Joanna Lumley as Pauline's upper-class former school friend Majorie Majors. Joanna hadn't really done much in recent years, to be honest, but as a result of her being in this film she walked into *Absolutely Fabulous*, the BBC comedy show with Jennifer Saunders, and hasn't looked back since.

Shirley, a middle-aged Liverpool housewife, finds herself talking to the wall while she prepares her husband's chips 'n' egg, wondering what happened to her life. She compares scenes in her current life with what she used to be like, and feels she's stagnated and in a rut. She yearns to drink "a glass of wine in the country where the grapes are grown." But when her best friend wins an all-expenses-paid vacation to Greece for two, Shirley begins to see the world, and herself, in a different light.

Pauline was perfect casting. She was an "ordinary-looking" woman, your typical housewife (no disrespect intended) and "nothing special."

But the idea was to prove that you don't have to be anything or anyone special in life; life is what you make of it.

The idea of a few weeks paid work in Greece really appealed to me too, and I particularly loved Lewis' way of working. He didn't rush about, he developed a nice steady pace and the unit worked brilliantly. We started off in Twickenham Studios (thus ensuring the actors weren't sun-tanned before they should be in the story) before going out to Mikonos. It was pretty hot out there, and I used to really look forward to the end of a working day when we'd go off for a swim in the cool ocean. Work doesn't get much better than this.

Pauline was Oscar-nominated (and won the BAFTA for Best Actress) and went on to a great career as a leading lady in films. I love her dearly and still keep in touch.

Reunion

I was next offered another TV production. It was called *Till We Meet Again* and produced by Steve Lanning. I remembered Steve as a production manager on *Watcher in the Woods.* Now he was producing, and fortunately remembered me! It was directed by Charles Jarrott, with whom I'd worked with a couple of years earlier on *The Barbara Hutton Story.*

I guess you'd call it a rites of passage sort of story, revolving around the lives of three young women as they deal with the incidents around them between 1913 and 1956. Of course, along the way they find romance and become swept up in family intrigue.

As with Charles' other show, a great cast was assembled. A lot of them were up-and-coming actors, and not that well known (then), but they are now: Hugh Grant, Courtenay Cox, Mia Sara, Lucy Gutteridge and also Michael York, Barry Bostwick and Juliet Mills.

It received good notices and rates as a very enjoyable drama, so see it if you get the chance.

Ssshhh

Secret Weapon was next. That was directed by Ian Sharp, whom I hadn't worked with before. He started off as a TV director on things like *The Professionals* and *Minder*, and then went on to direct *Who Dares Wins.* He was a very good action director.

Griffin Dunne, Jerome Krabbe, Brian Cox and John Rhys-Davies were amongst the cast; we shot Down Under in Australia with a bit in

Italy too if memory serves. It was about a Jewish man who'd obtained blueprints to a nuclear bomb in Israel and took them to Australia with him—this was the "Secret weapon" in the title. A really good dramatic-action film.

New York–Bound

Eve of Destruction saw me travel to New York again. That's always a bonus! I think we shot in L.A. too, which I'm not too keen on! Duncan Gibbons was the young director. It was his second film, and sadly a couple of years later he died in an horrendous fire. He was only 40.

An old friend from the home country on the film was production designer Peter Lamont. We'd worked on three Bond films together, so had a lot to talk about and catch up on which was great.

It was, I guess you'd say, a sort of sci-fi film with Gregory Hines and Renée Soutendijk, who played Eve.

It was all about a military robot that was created in the exact likeness of Eve, and was called Eve VIII. It was a bit like the *Terminator* idea. Anyway, this robot (which carries an armory, including a nuclear bomb) is sent out on a number of tests in the city. But things go wrong, and she starts developing a ruthless streak, turning into a killing machine whenever anyone gets in her way. Gregory Hines had to stop her.

It was an interesting film. The crew was largely American; I suppose there are a few differences in the approaches of the American and British way of making films, but essentially it is the same process and a film set in Tokyo, L.A., London or Toronto is much the same in feel and atmosphere. But I do admit to becoming increasingly more home sick as I got older. I missed my little garden, local golf course and village. This was 1990 and I was 66. It was in fact to be the last decade of my working life. I think my feelings were signifying it was probably getting to that crunch time when you'd happily forsake a 5 A.M. alarm call for a lie-in and lazy morning with the newspaper.

Stepping Out

Having said that, there are some films that come along that make you forget any idea of retiring and fuel you only with enthusiasm. For me, that came with *Stepping Out*.

Like *Shirley Valentine*, it had started out as a play, written by Richard Harris. It was set in a London church hall and was all about a bunch of left-footed suburbanites getting together for a charity dance gig. The play was on in Richmond Theatre at the time we were making *Shirley Valentine* and Richmond is only a short distance from Twickenham Studios. Allan Foenander, the casting director, implored John Dark and Lewis Gilbert to see the comedy. They did, and soon after put in a bid for the film rights. With *Shirley Valentine* being a great success, the American backers asked John what he was next planning to do. He told them about this play, and they readily agreed to back it, but did insist that casting approval lay with them. I think they felt their noses had been put out a bit when Lewis and John stood their ground over Pauline Collins rather than go with their suggestion (which I believe was Cher). Okay, it was a deal.

The story was transposed to Buffalo, New York, in an attempt to "Americanize" it and Richard Harris did a splendid job in adapting his play.

Casting began coming together. Liza Minnelli was announced as the lead character Mavis Turner, the former dancer whose job it was to whip the gang into shape. "The gang" were Julie Walters, Bill Irwin, Ellen Greene, Sheila McCarthy and Jane Krakowski, amongst others. Jane Krakowski has gone on to great success in *Ally McBeal* on TV since. Providing the musical accompaniment on piano was the wonderful Shelley Winters.

Although set in New York State, we actually set up production in Toronto, Canada. There are a great many tax incentives in Canada for filmmakers and, to be honest, this was the type of film that could have been shot anywhere. There were no specifics in the script, it was just "a location" in America. Buffalo was settled on as it was as good as any other!

It was wonderful to be working with Lewis Gilbert again and, although I've talked of the film being a "dance story," it was in fact a comedy which so happened to involve a bit of dancing, not the other way around.

The whole unit were brilliant. We had a small studio (which was a converted warehouse in fact), and it had a rather low roof. To achieve the desired lighting, I sometimes had to bounce lights off mirrors, as it was quite tricky otherwise.

Speaking of mirrors, photographing some of the dance routines proved interesting as, of course, there were a lot of full-length mirrors on the set which the dancers used to watch their movements and so on. I had to be careful so as not to get any lights or cameras in the mirrors. They had a great choreographer and so I knew how the dancers would move, and I was able to angle the mirrors (ten on one occasion) so as to not give the game away.

Liza was terrific and became a great friend. When I first met her, I was a bit concerned about how I would photograph her—always my first concern with my leading ladies. But she was delighted with the first few day's rushes and that sealed our friendship. Liza did have a lot of trouble with her hips, as most young dancers do in later life, and I know she had one leg slightly longer than the other which caused her to walk with

Top: Checking the light for his leading lady, Liza Minelli, during *Stepping Out*. *Bottom:* A load of bottoms! The cast wish Alan a happy birthday.

a small limp. But she moved in such a way that you'd never notice! She later had both hips replaced and went through some health scares but I'm so delighted to see that she's overcome everything. We kept in touch for many, many years and always looked forward to hearing from her.

Shelley Winters was a very distinguished actress with many wonderful credits to her name, but I soon discovered she has a great sense of humor and so there were never any problems with Shelley, only fun.

Birthday Boy

As I do each year, I had a birthday. It so happened to fall right in the middle of our schedule on the film, and unbeknownst to me all the girls had been conspiring behind my back. They wrote a little song about me and, on the morning of my birthday, danced on to the set singing this song. At the end they all turned around to show their rear ends and across them was written (one letter on each) my name! They then produced a cake too. It was one of the most memorable birthdays I have ever had. I know my wife Sheila was bowled over by it all too as she was made to feel a part of the "family," and so we both share some very fond memories of the picture and the lovely people involved.

XV

The Final Furlong

After *Stepping Out* I returned to Britain and worked on the last *Carry On* film the following year. After completing the five-week shoot, I was approached to work on a TV series called *Covington Cross*. One of the producers was my old friend Aida Young, and it sounded quite interesting.

Covington Cross was a fanciful drama about life in medieval England. Sir Thomas (Nigel Terry), a widower, has four children. Richard (Jonathan Firth) and Armus (Tim Killick) are stalwart young knights, but the other two children only wish they were. Cedric (Glen Quinn) is in training to be a cleric as his late mother wished. Eleanor (Ione Skye) finds it difficult because of her sex, although she is as good on a horse and with a crossbow as any man. (Another son, William, left for the Crusades after the pilot episode and was barely mentioned again.)

Sir Thomas has developed a relationship with Lady Elizabeth (Cherie Lunghi), who lives in her own nearby castle. Their other neighbor, Baron John Mullens (James Faulkner), is continually plotting to ruin Sir Thomas and take his land.

The series was filmed on location at Allington Castle and Penshurst Place in Kent.

There were 13 60-minute episodes with directors Herbie Wise, Peter Sasdy, Ian Toynton, William Deer, Alister Hallum, James Keach, Les Landau, Francis Megahy and Joe Napolitano. There were many guest stars too, among them Greg Wise, Julian Fellowes, James Nesbitt, Sabina Franklyn and Art Malik.

It was quite a long stint for me, and lovely to work with so many old friends. I'm not sure of the ins and outs of what happened, but only seven episodes ever aired (certainly in the U.S. in any event) even though

13 were completed. That's a shame, but I'm afraid these things happen when money is involved.

Geraldine

After a few weeks off, I heard about a new film that Rank was financing with Julie Walters. I grew very fond of Julie during *Stepping Out* and so the idea of working with her again appealed greatly to me.

It was a gentle comedy, directed by Christopher Monger and based on the novel *Geraldine, For the Love of a Transvestite*. So I assume you can get the drift of what it's about!

Adrian Pasdar played a 30-something American businessman in London, called Gerald. One day his wife arrived home earlier than expected and found all manner of ladies' clothing and underclothing spread around the bedroom. She immediately thought that Gerald was having an affair, threw him out and subsequently divorced him. He takes refuge in a rented room from landlady Monica (Julie Walters). Monica gets to know the strange lady who visits Gerald sometimes, but then realizes it *is* Gerald—he is a transvestite and is also known as Geraldine!

It's a warm story that deals with a tricky subject, and I know Adrian did struggle at times with the part. Julie Walters was a great support and so helpful to him.

H.E.A.T.

It was then back to TV, and back to America ... or South America; to be precise, Mexico. The show was called *Acapulco H.E.A.T.* and my goodness, it was hot down there. The temperature and humidity combined to make it unbearable at times and I absolutely hated it. I'd often leave my room at seven in the morning and by the time I reached the elevator some 25 yards away, I'd be perspiring. And that's early morning!

I had 22 one-hour episodes to get through though. Dear Sid Hayers was one of the six directors on the series, and that helped make it bearable to a certain extent. The local crew were very professional and good-humored, and that side of things worked well. One of the directors was a first-timer and pretty useless, particularly as he wouldn't take any help. It was certainly one of the toughest series I've ever done. It went to a second and third season, but I declined them.

It was nice to get home after six months in Mexico, back to my beloved garden and local golf course. I didn't do anything for the rest of

1993, and I suppose I was telling myself that it was all a bit bloody silly doing these long shoots that I found heavy going. They took a lot out of me and I was approaching 70; I ought to have been taking it easy not pushing myself through gruelling schedules.

The funny thing is that, when you decide to take a bit of time off, you get terribly twitchy if the phone doesn't ring! But then it did ring, and I found myself being offered a job that involved so many old friends that I just couldn't resist!

The Other Gerry

Gerry Anderson has long been a name associated with wonderful television series, such as *Thunderbirds, Captain Scarlet and the Mysterious, Joe 90* and *Terrahawks*. He was certainly a well-known and well-liked man in the business.

In the mid–1980s, he had the idea of producing a show which was part live action and part puppetry. It was called *Space Police* and he made a pilot show from his own resources; I was DoP for him over at Bray Studios. The show, for one reason or another, didn't progress to a series even though the idea and pilot was greeted with enthusiasm. I think part of the problem was that it fell between two stools: It was neither a children's nor adult show, but somewhere in between.

Quite a few years later, Gerry was involved in a little bit of work for Mentorn Productions when they asked him if he had any project ideas that might interest them. He, of course, suggested *Space Police* and showed them the pilot. It starred Shane Rimmer and Catherine Chavalier. They were enthusiastic, took it to Cannes and shortly afterwards it was all systems go.

There were a few changes. Firstly it was to be an adult-oriented show and totally live-action. And as there was American money involved, it had to cater to American audiences too. Twenty-four one-hour episodes were commissioned and a slew of American writers moved in—ten at one point. Unfortunately the name *Space Police* had since been registered by Lego and so we had to change it to *Space Precinct*.

As well as human cast members, there were to be a lot of aliens too; mainly prosthetic costumes with actors inside. That saw a major operation crank-up in the effects and make up departments. Masks were made from latex and facial muscles and eye movements were controlled remotely, and of course each alien required their own "operator" who had to be out of view but know every movement required. That became quite a logistical exercise.

Ted Shackleford and Rob Youngblood were cast as the male leads, and over 200 technicians were recruited. The production was split between Pinewood and Shepperton Studios, with the live-action being at Pinewood and the special effects at Shepperton. Some of the special effects models were fantastic. They stood up to six feet tall and were often covered in a smoke-filled haze; that made it a tricky job for the boys on there day in and day out.

We had a great gang of directors come on board: My old mates John Glen and Sid Hayers, along with Piers Haggard, Alan Birkinshaw, Colin Bucksey, Peter Duffell and Jim Goddard. Like the old days on *The Avengers,* it was all bang-bang-bang. We had ten shooting days and a budget of £1 million per episode. The digital effects (which were then really only just coming into the affordable domain) used a great chunk of that money.

I was DoP, along with Tony Spratling, and between us we brought the series in on time and created a good-looking program. It was often difficult working on the sets because we had mezzanine floors built so that a greater number of sets could be accommodated on each stage. That often meant that, when I was on the top floor, there was very little space between me and the ceiling, which made lighting it tricky and, indeed, very hot for the actors. You can imagine, particularly in the summer months, how unbearable it became at times. But we didn't have the luxury of being able to stop, we had to carry on and, in the best tradition, did.

I know that Gerry had battles of his own too, as the money didn't come through as it should and it was often a case of it arriving at the eleventh hour, or even after that, when large debts were beginning to run up. But Gerry never let any of the money worries overshadow the production. It all came through in the end, and I think we delivered 24 hours of excellent entertainment. Along the way we had some great guest stars: Steven Berkoff, Burt Kwouk, Maryam d'Abo, Christopher Fairbank and Ray Winstone.

Sadly, the critics weren't too kind and the transmission time of the show, 6 P.M. on BBC2, became a grave error of judgment on the schedulers' part. They saw it as a Gerry Anderson production, like say *Thunderbirds* was. It wasn't a children's show, it was an adult show which would have been better served with an eight or nine P.M. broadcast, when the adults were home from work and had eaten their dinner.

Native

Return of the Native was a telefilm of Thomas Hardy's famous novel of the same name. Jack Gold telephoned me to say he would be directing it, and was I available? Well, he was another old mate and although I'd told myself I should retire, I couldn't help but want to work with Jack again because I knew it would be an enjoyable experience. I'm so pleased I agreed as we had a truly terrific cast, including a young actress named Catherine Zeta-Jones, who was really just beginning to make a name for herself (she is now, of course, Mrs. Michael Douglas). Then there was Clive Owen, who has had great success in recent years, and the ever-brilliant Joan Plowright.

Catherine was such a beautiful girl, and such a pleasure to light. I did actually say to her that I felt she would go far in the business. It was just a gut feeling, and when you've been around as long as I have, you tend to get an idea of the actors with "star quality."

That was quite a challenging shoot because of all the location work and tight schedule. You know what the British weather can be like; we'd film one sequence in blistering sunshine one day, and the next day go back to complete the piece and it'd be gray and overcast. So I had to keep all my wits about me!

It was as though all my old mates were suddenly very busy and determined to stop me from retiring, as no sooner had I completed *Return of the Native* than the phone rang again and Ian Toynton (with whom I'd last worked on *Space Precinct*) said he was making a U.S. telefilm called *Annie: A Royal Adventure*. It was a sort of follow-up to the film *Annie* in which Albert Finney was so wonderful. In this story, Joan Collins and George Hearn were the adult leads, and Ashley Johnson played the now-more-mature Annie. I don't think it was what you'd call a must-see show, but as always we had a great deal of fun. The last time I'd worked with Joan was several decades earlier on one of her very first films. She was a different Joan Collins from when I remembered her, and much grander. I reminded her how we'd worked together all those years ago and she said, "I don't wish to know that, thank you very much." She looked, and still looks, absolutely fantastic but perhaps she thought I was having a dig at her and showing up her age! It was, in fact, a perfectly innocent remark. Ah well, never mind.

Spooky

There was a popular series on HBO in America called *Tales from the Crypt*. I suppose it was a bit like *The Twilight Zone* and *Alfred Hitchcock Presents* and other shows in that vein. They were all half-hour stories, with more than 90 being produced, between 1989 and 1996. A few were made over here, at Ealing Studios, and I was asked to work on two of the episodes: *Last Respects* and *The Kidnapper*.

My old chum Freddie Francis was directing the first one, and requested I work as his DoP. Freddie is an Oscar-winning cinematographer, as well as a director, and so he knows his stuff. But I'd known Freddie for so many years, and knew him as a good friend, that there weren't any doubts in my mind we'd work well together and he wouldn't try to tell me my job or criticize me. He never did either.

One story was of a pawnbroker who falls in love with a pregnant girl. After the child is born, he gets jealous and plans to kidnap the child to get it out of the way. After the abduction, his girlfriend becomes intolerable to live with. It was better when the baby was there! He then tries to buy the child back from the people he hired to kidnap her, but it's no use. He then decides to "steal" another woman's child ... only to learn that it was his ex-girlfriend's child!

The second, an equally moralistic story, starred dear Emma Samms, whom I'd worked with on her first film, *Arabian Adventure*. It was about Dorles, Marlys and Lavone, three sisters who think they have found a way out of all their troubles. They discover a monkey's paw that grants them their wishes. Soon they learn the penalty of the wishes they make.

All good stuff.

Well, it was 1997. I'd had a few months off and was contemplating retirement (again). The business was changing, people were putting in very long hours. It wasn't so much the work, but the getting up at 5 A.M. and getting home at 9 P.M. that was beginning to take its toll on me. I loved the work, but was feeling my age a bit I suppose.

Under the Sea

But when you're asked to do a film with a director even older than yourself, who shows nothing but enthusiasm and determination, you think to yourself, "Well, okay, maybe just one more film then." That director was Michael Anderson and the film was *20,000 Leagues Under the Sea* for Hallmark. I had known Michael for half a century. He was an assistant director at Denham when I was starting out in the business, and so there was a fair bit of history between us.

It was perhaps one of the most joyous films I'd worked on.

Originally it was said we were going to film in the Red Sea and on the great tank in Malta, but the budget wouldn't quite stretch and so the film was based out of Pinewood and we made terrific use of the outdoor water tank there, along with many of the stages which had internal tanks. I defy anyone to watch it and say that was all on the paddock tank and not at sea though!

We had to film a lot of water-based sequences, but the camera never went underwater at all. We did tricky things like shooting through a tank (as in *For Your Eyes Only*) complete with bubbles, and the actors would be the other side of it creating the effect that they were walking under water! That's the magic of movies.

There were lots of sequences with the submarine *Nautilus* coming up out of the water; we used the deep end of the paddock tank for that, with rigs and wave machines. Then we'd have mirror-paper across the "portholes" and play around with the light as though it was all underwater. Of course, submarines are quite confined space-wise and again I had to think about how to light the sets. Much was improbable, but nothing was impossible!

After this film, I made a conscious decision that it was time to step aside and let some of the younger guys and girls have a go. I'd had the most fantastic career and was barely ever out of work throughout it. There aren't many people who can say that in this business. And I think it's better to decide to retire, rather than let the industry retire you!

XVI

The Business Nowadays

Although I'm now retired, it doesn't mean I don't take an interest in the business any more. I am still a member of the British Society of Cinematographers and as such attend their various lunches and screenings. It's a good opportunity to catch up with old friends and colleagues. I am also sometimes asked for advice from newcomers in the business and am often asked for interviews for fan magazines and the like—particularly with *Carry On,* Bond and *Star Wars.* I'm very flattered to be asked. I used to say that I haven't anything of much interest to share, but in taking the decision to sit down and commit some of my memories to paper, with this book, I've realized that there are a lot of stories and memories. Some important, some funny and some pointless—but interesting all the same.

One thing I did want to do was make it all interesting for the "average reader." I'm sure there are a few who be interested in the technicalities of lighting a set and where I put the camera on such and such a film, but I know that the interesting stories are more about the people, the locations and the stories.

However, I can't write a book about being a director of photography without a little bit of technical insight, so I thought the most interesting angle would be to take a brief look at how technology has changed over the years and the wonderful advances we've made.

Film

When I first started off, the film stock we used was typically 100 ASA daylight and 64 Tungsten, which was very slow compared to today when they have 500 and 800 ASA speed film, so you imagine then that night shooting for instance was much more difficult as the film wasn't as sensitive. So you'd need a lot of lighting despite it being night!

For day exterior shooting, one had to use a color correction filter which slowed the film down by approximately one stop. So when the daylight was poor, it wasn't possible to shoot because of lack of exposure.

Nowadays, the film stocks are much faster, with higher resolution, and you don't need to filter the difference between tungsten and daylight.

Lenses and Lighting

There was no such thing as a zoom lens when I first started!

There were a great many lenses around and you'd have to know which was best suited to what purpose.

The zoom lens came in around the mid–60s. It was quite restrictive in the early days as there was a problem with speed. The widest aperture was F4. To light an F2 aperture you'd need a 100-foot candle, for F4 you'd need four 100-foot candles. So shooting on F2 you'd have a small light switch to a zoom lens and you need much bigger lights. What developed from the added need for light, was the use of reflective light. You can't always have too many lights on a small set, so what we did was have lights around the set and have big white screens to bounce the light into the areas that were tricky to get lights themselves into. It looked softer and worked wonderfully well. That became the vogue. It was called "bounced light." If you had an open ceiling set, you'd often put a white screen up there and bounce light into the set.

CinemaScope and VistaVision

You'll have heard of these techniques. CinemaScope used an anamorphic lens which stretched the picture sideways, two and a half times, and then squeezed it onto 35mm film. When projected, it needed a lens to "unsqueeze" the image and project it on to the screen. The ratio was about 2.5 (wide) to 1 (height). It revolutionized cinema by offering "widescreen" options, fitting much more into the frame. True, it could be misused and lose "intimacy" in some cases, but it's here to stay!

VistaVision was almost 35mm size without employing 70mm techniques or film. What you did was run the film sideways through the camera, so it produced a CinemaScope-type picture without an anamorphic lens. You'd need a special lens on a projector though. Up until recently, as far as I'm aware, VistaVision was still employed in filming plates for back projection in movies, as the image wasn't squeezed as it might be with CinemaScope, and the quality was superb.

Computers

When I started, there was nothing other than what we could do in the camera and optically, or with miniature in post-production. Nowadays computers have revolutionalized the business with CGI (Computer Graphic Imagery) technology and capabilities. On *Space Precinct* we had a lot of computer work adding in the effects, which although expensive was considerably easier and less time-consuming for us on the stage floor shooting, and that made me think then. Gone were the time-consuming optical effects, foreground miniatures and the like. Of course, they still have their place as these methods are sometimes simpler and easier to employ, but when you look at today's big productions and audience expectations, we have to get bigger and better each time.

I look at what George Lucas has achieved in the last 25 years and it amazes me. Now of course, digital technology is coming to the fore. Just as CDs "replaced" vinyl, DVDs will do so with video and digital recording will replace film. That's for sure.

Changes

People ask me if the business has changed over the last 50 years. Well, as far as production is involved, no it hasn't. Sure there are new techniques, but I could walk into any film studio in the world and feel at home. Perhaps the people who run the business have changed and with bigger expenditure comes a different attitude. But to be a good cinematographer, all you need is a vision. Don't be too concerned about the technology, I say; think about your vision and the rest will fall into place. That's why you employ special effects experts. I daresay, just as I couldn't operate a computer, they couldn't light a film set. We shouldn't be afraid of new technology; we should embrace it and work together.

BSC

I keep up to date with advances through some of the trade magazines and, in particular, via the BSC. Up until now I haven't mentioned our society (to give it its proper name, the British Society of Cinematographers), a very important body.

Most DoPs are members, but it's not something you can apply for—you're invited to join. It's quite an honor in fact, and one I gratefully accepted a few decades ago.

It was in 1947 that Bert Easey, then head of the Denham and Pinewood studio camera departments and the man who gave me my initial break, first put forward the idea of forming a society of British cinematographers. Most of Britain's distinguished cameramen were gathered for an industry dinner at the Orchard Hotel in Ruislip, West London. Among the enthusiastic diners that night were such behind-the-camera luminaries as Georges Perinal, Desmond Dickinson, Guy Green, Robert Krasker, Harry Waxman, Otto Heller, George Hill, Jack Hildyard, Alex Tozer, Gordon Craig, and Max Green, plus many other leading cameramen and representatives of various camera departments. Bert Easey's vision was that it would be a non-political guild or society, made up of feature production cameramen in the U.K., based along similar lines to that of the prestigious American Society of Cinematographers which had been formed in 1919. With the enthusiastic approval of the assembled gathering, the British Society of Cinematographers Limited was born in September 1949. The 55 original members were each issued with a small share and their objectives were fourfold:

To promote and encourage the pursuit of the highest standards in the craft of Motion Picture Photography.

To further the applications by others of the highest standards in the craft of Motion Picture Photography and to encourage original and outstanding work.

To co-operate with all whose aims and interests are wholly or in part related to those of the society.

To provide facilities for social intercourse between the members and arrange lectures, debates and meetings calculated to further the objects of the Society.

Freddie Young, at the time chief cameraman at MGM in Borehamwood, took the chair as the first president. Bert Easey was elected secretary and treasurer. Guy Green took on the role of vice-president and Jack Cardiff, Lovat Cave Chinn, Desmond Dickinson and Derick Williams were elected to the board.

Initially, the Society's meetings were held at the Orchard where the management curtained off a room. When the Orchard was refurbished, board meetings rotated around governor's homes every six weeks. Many tales have passed down about these early meetings. Ossie Morris said that in the early days, the meetings used to start with a drink and a sandwich;

but as time went on these were replaced by a sumptuous four-course dinner provided by the governors' wives.

Unfortunately, this meant that the actual business rarely got going before 10:30 or 11 o'clock and often didn't finish until one or two in the morning. Although the dinners were most enjoyable, it was very hard on the wives and was certainly impractical for those board members who had to be at the studios for early starts.

It was decided to move them to weekends and these continued at Pinewood and Rank Labs until 1990.

That year, through the auspices of Shepperton chief Denis Carrigan, the Society acquired an elegant club room, situated in the Old House where the corridors and meeting room display photographs of presidents and the honor boards listing the achievements of past and present members. One of the early secretaries of the BSC was Joan Calvert. She took over the post from her boss at Technicolor, George Gunn, in 1967 and later, when Bert Easey died in 1973, she twinned that with the job of treasurer until she retired from the industry in 1979.

On December 7, 1951, the Cinematographers held the first of its celebrated Operator Nights. The Orchard at Ruislip was the venue and the cost to attend that first function was just one guinea (or, in current money, £1.05). It was introduced to give DoPs the opportunity to express their gratitude to their operators.

Over the years it has developed into one of the Society's most successful annual functions and currently has a regular December slot at Pinewood Studios. The Operator's Night is also the occasion when the Society hands out its prizes for the year. The first among these was the Bert Easey Technical Award, named in honor of Bert's tireless energy and unflagging enthusiasm that brought about the birth of the BSC. The award is a gift of the Board and only given to an individual or company who has contributed something outstanding in the way of endeavor or equipment. The initial award went to George Ashworth, Chief Engineer, Denham and Pinewood Studios, for outstanding work in designing and perfecting a beam splitter camera which advanced the technique of the travelling matte process. Over the years it has been bestowed on companies such as Lee Filters, Arnold and Richter, Eastman Kodak, the House of Samuelson and Rank Taylor Hobson for their cinematographic contributions. Talented individuals including Wally Weevers, Denys Coop, Les Ostinelli and Jean Pierre Beauviala of AATON are among those who have also been honored.

Two years later, the BSC Best Cinematography award was inaugurated and voted on by the entire membership. Its first recipient was Ossie Morris for John Huston's "*Moulin Rouge*." His award was a silver tankard. Later, Academy Award–winning production designer Ken

Adam was invited to design a futuristic golden camera for the annual winners.

Each year the name of the winner of the Best Cinematography award is engraved on a plaque on the Society's Golden Camera, a magnificent model of the celebrated Mitchell N C Camera, crafted by renowned Pinewood camera engineer George Ashworth, a veteran of the first-ever meeting of the Society.

The model is on view in the main reception at Pinewood Studios, traditional home of the Society, and always comes out for the Society's major events. Among the multiple winners of the BSC Cinematography Award are Freddie Young, Ossie Morris, Douggie Slocombe and Freddie Francis. In later years, the award included several foreign DoPs: Sven Nykvist, Philippe Rousselot, Vittorio Storaro, Pierre L'Homme, Janus Kaminski, Dante Spinotti and Conrad Hall.

In recent years, Arri has also contributed to the Operators evening by sponsoring an award in memory of John Alcott, BSC, who won many awards for his work on *Barry Lyndon* and died tragically at a young age. This is given to the person who, in the opinion of the board, has con-

Alan with camera.

tributed most towards perpetuating the original aims of the Society. Past winners include Les Ostinelli, BSC, Peter Newbrook, BSC, Wolfgang Suschitzky, BSC, Eric Cross, BSC, A.A. Englander, BSC, Ossie Morris, BSC, Paul Beeson, BSC, Harvey Harrison, BSC, Alex Thomson, BSC, Joe Dunon, BSC, Michael Samuelson, BSC, Robin Vidgeon, BSC, Frances Russell and, in all modesty, me.

Until recent years, Ladies Night was an annual "black tie" event with the idea that DoPs could entertain their wives with a dinner and dance to make up for the time spent on location. For nearly 25 years this was held at the Savoy Hotel. Honored guests over the years included such celebrated names as Sir John Mills, Sir Dirk Bogarde, Otto Preminger and Peter Sellers. The third and most recent annual function in the Society's calendar is the BSC Summer Luncheon. First held in 1987, in the conservatory at Shepperton Studios, to honor the founder and veteran members of the Society, it proved such a success that a similar lunch had to be organized the following year to thank the Society's patron members. In 1989 it marked the Society's 40th anniversary and has now become an important summer gathering of cameramen, patrons and friends.

I'm proud to be a part of it.

Breaking In

I'm quite often get asked how you "break into the business" nowadays. I wish there was a set answer. There isn't.

All I would say is develop a flair for photography. Be it stills, video or Super 8mm even. Learn about light, get a feel for how you can use the light and for processing.

It might be a romanticized piece of career advice as I know it's very difficult nowadays because there isn't the continuity of production in this country as there was in the '50s and '60s. Producers would make two or three films a year. Now it's a film every five years maybe. It is tough, but my advice is learn from the floor. It gives you the best grounding ever. If you're passionate enough, you will do it.

If I could, you can.

Filmography

This filmography is in two parts: those works for which I was a cinematographer, and those for which I had any other duty.

As Cinematographer

20,000 Leagues Under the Sea (1997) (TV)

Dir: Michael Anderson
Lp: Richard Crenna, Ben Cross, Julie Cox

Television mini-series based on the classic Jules Verne undersea adventure.

Tales from the Crypt (1996) (TV Series)

episode "Last Respects"
Dir: Freddie Francis
Lp: Emma Samms, Kerry Fox, Julie Cox

Three crazy sisters get their hands on a magical monkey's paw that can grant three wishes to its owner. The bad thing, is the wishes all turn out to be fatal. So they have to try to outsmart it by wording the wishes carefully.

episode "Kidnapper"
Dir: Freddie Francis
Lp: Steve Coogan, Julia Sawalha, Serena Gordon

A slightly unbalanced shop keeper falls in love with a pregnant young woman who enters his shop one night. She moves in with him, but only as a friend. He doesn't seem to comprehend that she doesn't want to be his girlfriend and tries to make her change her mind. When she has the baby, he can't stand how much attention the infant requires, so he has the baby kidnapped by a sleazy baby broker. The young woman goes insane due to the loss of the baby, and the man decides that the only way to help her is to kidnap another baby. He snatches a baby from a woman in a public park and gets caught by an angry mob. Just before he is beaten to death by the mob, he discovers that the baby he tried to steal was really his girlfriend's baby all along.

Annie: A Royal Adventure! (1995) (TV)
Dir: Ian Toynton
Lp: Ashley Johnson, Joan Collins, Ian McDiarmid
Heart-warming family tale of little orphan Annie and an adventure in London.

The Return of the Native (1994) (TV)
Dir: Jack Gold
Lp: Catherine Zeta-Jones, Clive Owen, Ray Stevenson, Joan Plowright
Thomas Hardy's classic about how a village girl returns after years abroad to wreck havoc with the local men!

Space Precinct (1994) (TV Series)
Dir: Sid Hayers, John Glen, Piers Haggard, Alan Birkinshaw, Colin Bucksey, Peter Duffell, Jim Goddard
Lp: Ted Shackleford, Rob Youngblood, Nancy Paul
Gerry Anderson's first live-action, adult series about the "Space Police."

Acapulco H.E.A.T. (1993) (TV Series)
Dir: Sid Hayers, Michael Hofstein, Frank Morehead, Harry Ambrose, Kevin James Dobson, Henri Safran
Lp: Catherine Oxenburg, Brendan Kelly, Alison Armitage
Ashley, formerly of MI6, and Mike Savage, formerly of the CIA, are co-leaders of the H.E.A.T. team, a group of specialists recruited to fight a secret war against international terrorism. Based in Puerto Vallarta, Mexico, the team operates throughout the Caribbean and around the world behind the unlikely cover of being the owners and models for a fashion company specializing in beach wear.

Covington Cross (1992) (TV Series)
Dir: William Dear, Alister Hallum, James Keach, Les Landau, Francis Megahy, Joe Napolitano, Peter Sasdy, Ian Toynton, Herbert Wise
Lp: Nigel Terry, Colin Firth, Peter Brooke
Following the adventures and loves of the children of an English Lord during the Middle Ages.

Carry On Columbus (1992)
Dir: Gerry Thomas
Lp: Jim Dale, Bernard Cribbins, Julian Clary, Sara Crowe
How Christopher Columbus discovered the Americas—according to the Carry On gang!

Just Like a Woman (1992)
Dir: Christopher Monger
Lp: Julie Walters, Adrian Pasdar, Paul Freeman
An American living in London moves into lodgings after his wife throws him out, and reveals to his landlady that he is a transvestite.
Critics: "A tepid comedy of Anglo-Saxon inhibition"—*The Observer*

Stepping Out (1991)

Dir: Lewis Gilbert

Lp: Liza Minnelli, Julie Walters, Shelley Winters

A tap dance teacher takes on a bunch of amateurs and has to train them up for a charity show.

Eve of Destruction (1991)

Dir: Duncan Gibbins

Lp: Gregory Hines, Renée Soutendijk, Michael Green

Eve is a military robot made to look exactly like her creator. When she is Damaged during a bank robbery, the robot begins to use more of the dark memories with which she has been programmed by her creator. She will become a killing machine if anyone tries to stop her.

Secret Weapon (1990) (TV)

Dir: Ian Sharp

Lp: Griffin Dunne, Karen Allen, Jerome Krabbé, John Rhys Davies

A Jewish man obtains blueprints to a nuclear bomb in Israel and takes them to Australia.

Till We Meet Again (1989) (mini) (TV Series)

Dir: Charles Jarrott

Lp: Michael York, Courtenay Cox, Mia Sara, Lucy Gutteridge, Hugh Grant

TV movie revolving around the lives of three young women as they deal with the world around them. Along the way they find romance and become swept up in family intrigue.

Shirley Valentine (1989)

Dir: Lewis Gilbert

Lp: Pauline Collins, Tom Conti, Bernard Hill

A bored housewife abandons her suburban life and husband for a holiday romance in Greece.

Critics: "Enjoyable, old fashioned movie with some entertaining monologues"—Halliwell's

The Tenth Man (1988) (TV)

Dir: Jack Gold

Lp: Anthony Hopkins, Kristin Scott Thomas, Derek Jacobi

Based on the novel of the same name, by Graham Greene this is the story of French advocate Chavel who, while imprisoned by the Germans during the Occupation, trades his material possessions for his life with another prisoner when condemned to the firing squad.

Jack the Ripper (1988) (TV)

Dir: David Wickes

Lp: Michael Caine, Lewis Collins, Armand Assante

Lavish television adaptation of the famous 1888 murders in London's East End by a notorious killer dubbed "Jack the Ripper."

Without a Clue (1988)
Dir: Thom Eberhardt
Lp: Michael Caine, Ben Kingsley

The story of Sherlock Holmes ... or rather the story of how detective John Watson created 'Sherlock Holmes' and then employed a failing actor to impersonate the character.

A Fish Called Wanda (1988)
Dir: Charles Crichton
Lp: John Cleese, Jamie Lee Curtis, Kevin Kline, Michael Palin

A superior diamond heist comedy focusing on greed and double-crossing.

Poor Little Rich Girl: The Barbara Hutton Story (1987) (TV)
Dir: Charles Jarrott
Lp: Farrah Fawcett, Burl Ives, Brenda Blethyn

Biopic about Barbara Hutton, heiress to the immense Woolworth store fortune. She was married eight times; Cary Grant was one of her husbands.

Hearts of Fire (1987)
Dir: Richard Marquand
Lp: Bob Dylan, Rupert Everett, Fiona Flanagan, Julian Glover

A female rock singer succeeds with the help of a reclusive star and weary British rocker.

Critics: "Tedious exposé of the world of rock music, lacking in excitement and a sad end to Marquand's career—who died soon after finishing it."—Halliwell's

The Second Victory (1986)
Dir: Gerry Thomas
Lp: Anthony Andrews, Mario Adorf, Helmut Greim

A story of British Occupational forces in post–World War II Austria.

Lifeforce (1985)
Dir: Tobe Hooper
Lp: Steve Railsback, Peter Firth, Frank Finlay, Patrick Stewart.

Zombies from outer space wreak havoc in London.

Critics: "The unintentional laugh-fest of the season"—Variety.

A View to a Kill (1985)
Dir: John Glen
Lp: Roger Moore, Christopher Walken, Grace Jones

A megalomaniac villain is intent on destroying Silicon Valley. Agent 007 is sent in to save the day.

John and Yoko: A Love Story (1985) (TV)
Dir: Sandor Stern
Lp: Mark McGann, Kim Miyori

The lives of John Lennon and Yoko Ono, from before their first meeting to their rise to stardom.

Runaway Train (1985)

Dir: Andrei Konchalovsky

Lp: Jon Voight, Eric Roberts, Rebecca DeMornay

Escaped prisoners in the Alaskan wilderness commandeer a train, unaware that it can't stop.

Critics: "Nervy, exciting violence; immaculate, metallic camerawork; unstoppable pace."—Sight and Sound

Supergirl (1984)

Dir: Jeannot Szwarc

Lp: Helen Slater, Faye Dunaway, Peter O'Toole, Mia Farrow, Peter Cook.

When a Krypton power source falls into the hands of a power-hungry witch, Supergirl (Superman's cousin) is sent to retrieve it.

Octopussy (1983)

Dir: John Glen

Lp: Roger Moore, Maud Adams, Louis Jourdan, Steven Berkoff

James Bond goes in pursuit of a renegade Russian General intent on World War III.

Star Wars: Episode VI—Return of the Jedi (1983)

Dir: Richard Marquand

Lp: Mark Hamill, Harrison Ford, Carrie Fisher

The final installment in the Star Wars franchise.

Critics: "I admire the exquisite skill and talent which has been poured into these films, while finding the concepts behind these gigantic video games in the sky mindlessly tedious."—*Daily Mail*

The Hunchback of Notre Dame (1982) (TV)

Dir: Michael Tuchner

Lp: Anthony Hopkins, Lesley-Anne Down

A television movie adaptation of the famous love story.

Eye of the Needle (1981)

Dir: Richard Marquand

Lp: Donald Sutherland, Christopher Cazanove, Kate Nelligan

A superior thriller set during WWII on a tiny Scottish island. Germany's top spy has important information about the Allied forces and ends up on Storm Island after being shipwrecked trying to make a rendezvous with a U-Boat.

For Your Eyes Only (1981)

Dir: John Glen

Lp: Roger Moore, Julian Glover, Topol, Carol Bouquet

When the ATAC defence system carrying St George's spy ship is sunk, it becomes a race against time to prevent it falling into enemy hands.

Caveman (1981)

Dir: Carl Gottlieb

Lp: Ringo Starr, Dennis Quaid, Barbara Bach

Comic adventures of prehistoric man.

Critics: "Worth half an hour of anyone's time. Unfortunately the film runs 97 minutes."—*The Guardian*

The Watcher in the Woods (1980)
Dir: John Hough
Lp: Bette Davis, Carroll Baker, David McCallum

The teenage daughter of an American composer has strange and supernatural experiences in the British countryside.

Bear Island (1979)
Dir: Richard Marquand
Lp: Venessa Redgrave, Lloyd Bridges, Donald Sutherland, Richard Widmark

Meteorological experts on an Arctic island are menaced by neo–Nazis.

Birth of the Beatles (1979)
Dir: Richard Marquand
Lp: Stephen MacKenna, Rod Culbertson, John Altman, Ray Ashcroft, Ryan Michael.

The early days of the world-famous pop group.

The Legacy (1979)
Dir: Richard Marquand
Lp: Katharine Ross, Sam Elliott, Roger Daltrey

An American designer goes to stay with her employer and finds herself in the middle of a cult murder plot.

Arabian Adventure (1979)
Dir: Kevin Connor
Lp: Christopher Lee, Milo O'Shea, Emma Samms, Mickey Rooney

Flying carpets and "Open Sesames" in a family adventure in the vein of the Arabian Knights.

Warlords of Atlantis (1978)
Dir: Kevin Connor
Lp: Doug McClure, Peter Gilmore, Shane Rimmer

Victorian sea scientists discover a lost land underneath the Mediterranean.

Carry On Emmannuelle (1978)
Dir: Gerry Thomas
Lp: Kenneth Williams, Joan Sims, Peter Butterworth, Suzanne Dando

The raunchiest entry in the Carry On series, taking a pop at the Sylvia Kristel movies.

The Amsterdam Kill (1977)
Dir: Robert Clouse
Lp: Robert Mitchum, Bradford Dillman, Leslie Nielsen

An ex–DEA officer tries to protect a friend caught up in the Hong Kong drug wars.

Above: On location in Tuscany for *Return of the Jedi*. *Below:* Alan in costume for his big part, with Donald Sutherland.

The People That Time Forgot (1977)

Dir: Kevin Connor

Lp: Patrick Wayne, Sarah Douglas, Doug McClure, Shane Rimmer

Major McBride (Wayne) attempts to rescue an old friend who disappeared on a prehistoric island.

Checkered Flag or Crash (1977)

Dir: Alan Gibson

Lp: Joe Don Baker, Susan Sarandon, Larry Hagman

An off-road racing action story. Baker stars as "Walkaway" Madden, a hard-core racer whose "crash or win" attitude brings him into conflict with his fellow racers. Sarandon is a journalist in the George Plimpton mode, out to get the inside view of a 1000-mile race held in the Philippines.

Gulliver's Travels (1977)

Dir: Peter Hunt

Lp: Richard Harris

Retelling of the famous tale in which only Gulliver is human—the Lilliputians are animated.

Wombling Free (1977)

Dir: Lionel Jeffries

Lp: David Tomlinson, Frances de la Tour

Big screen outing for Wimbledon's furry litter collectors.

At the Earth's Core (1976)

Dir: Kevin Connor

Lp: Peter Cushing, Doug McClure

A scientist creates a giant drilling device to venture to the center of the Earth.

Trial by Combat (1976)

Dir: Kevin Connor

Lp: Donald Pleasence, John Mills

A secret society of medieval knights dedicate themselves to the ritual execution of criminals who escaped the law.

The Land That Time Forgot (1975)

Dir: Kevin Connor

Lp: Doug McClure, Susan Penhaligon, John McEnery

In 1916, survivors from a torpedoed supply ship find themselves on a legendary island full of prehistoric monsters.

Cleopatra Jones and the Casino of Gold (1975)

Dir: Chuck Bail

Lp: Tamara Dobson, Stella Stevens, Albert Popwell

A tough government female agent goes to Hong Kong to smash a drug ring.

Doug McClure heads the cast on *The Land That Time Forgot.*

Confessions of a Pop Performer (1975)

Dir: Norman Cohen
Lp: Robin Askwith, Anthony Booth, Doris Hare, Ian Lavender

A window cleaner joins a pop band and ends up bedding seemingly every woman he meets.

Visions of Eight (1973) (segment "The Fastest")

Dir: Kon Ichikawa

Olympic documentary focussing on eight topics: The Fastest, The Decathlon, The Losers, The Beginning, The Highest, The Women, The Longest, The Strongest.

The Legend of Hell House (1973)

Dir: John Hough
Lp: Pamela Franklin, Roddy McDowall, Clive Revill

Four people arrive at a haunted house where, previously, several psychic investigators have died.

Critics: "One of the most absorbing, goose fleshing and mind-pleasing ghostbreaker yarns on film."—Judith Crist

Carry On Girls (1973)

Dir: Gerry Thomas
Lp: Sid James, Joan Sims, Bernard Bresslaw

Fircombe, a wet, boring seaside resort, attempts to boost tourism with a beauty contest.

From Beyond the Grave (1973)
Dir: Kevin Connor
Lp: Peter Cushing, Donald Pleasence, Richard Todd

Episodic film with the proprietor of an East End antique shop involving his customers in horrific situations.

Not Now Darling (1973)
Dir: Ray Cooney
Lp: Leslie Phillips, Ray Cooney, Joan Sims

A furrier gets into a complicated situation after arranging for his mistress to have a cheap mink coat.

Bless This House (1972)
Dir: Gerry Thomas
Lp: Sid James, Diana Coupland, Peter Butterworth

Big screen treatment of the successful TV sitcom.

Carry On Abroad (1972)
Dir: Gerry Thomas
Lp: Sid James, Kenneth Williams, Charles Hawtrey, Hattie Jacques

It's all off to Ells Belles for a summer holiday with the gang.

For the Love of Ada (1972)
Dir: Harry Driver
Lp: Irene Handl, Wilfred Pickles

TV spinoff movie about an elderly grave digger and his wife celebrating their first wedding anniversary.

Critics: "A boneless jelly of a film, setting up pointless little heartbreaks so that it can dissolve them into a flood of cold sentimentality"—*Monthly Film Bulletin*

Carry On Henry (1971)
Dir: Gerry Thomas
Lp: Sid James, Kenneth Williams, Terry Scott, Joan Sims

Henry VIII gets the *Carry On* treatment.

Zeppelin (1971)
Dir: Etienne Périer
Lp: Michael York, Elke Sommer, Marius Goring

In 1915, the British attempt to steal secrets from the zeppelin works in Friedrichshafen.

Shirley's World (1971) (TV Series)
Prod: Lew Grade, Sheldon Lanning
Lp: Shirley MacLaine, John Gregson

To date, Shirley MacLaine's only television series. She plays a globetrotting photographer for a glossy magazine.

The Last Grenade (1970)

Dir: Gordon Flemyng
Lp: Stanley Baker, Honor Blackman, Richard Attenborough, Julian Glover

An army mercenary is betrayed by an ex-friend in the Congo, and pursues him to Hong Kong.

Perfect Friday (1970)

Dir: Peter Hall
Lp: Stanley Baker, Ursula Howells, David Warner

A bank manager engages aristocratic help to rob his own bank.

Captain Nemo and the Underwater City (1969)

Dir: James Hill
Lp: Robert Ryan, Chuck Connors, Bill Fraser, Kenneth Connor

Six survivors from an Atlantic shipwreck are picked up by a mysterious submarine and have adventures in a spectacular underwater city.

Mister Jerico (1969) (TV)

Dir: Sid Hayers
Lp: Patrick Macnee, Connie Stevens, Herbert Lom, Paul Darrow

Malta-set action-heist story.

The Last Grenade cinema poster.

Father Dear Father (1972)

Dir: William G. Stewart

Lp: Patrick Cargill, Natasha Pyne, Ann Holoway, Noel Dyson, Donald Sinden

A divorced middle-aged writer decides he should get married to help with his two teenage daughters' upbringing.

Critics: "Trivial comedy based on a TV sitcom, and looking and sounding like it."—Halliwell's

The Bofors Gun (1968)

Dir: Jack Gold

Lp: Nicol Williamson, John Thaw, David Warner, Ian Holm

In 1954 Germany, a British Army unit runs into trouble when a violent and unstable Irish private picks on a weakly National Service corporal.

Carry On Doctor (1968)

Dir: Gerry Thomas

Lp: Sid James, Frankie Howerd, Kenneth Williams

Hospital mayhem and madness with the gang.

Critics: "Usual unabashed mixture of double meanings, down to earth vulgarity, blue jokes"—*Variety*

Don't Lose Your Head (1967)

Dir: Gerry Thomas

Lp: Jim Dale, Sid James, Kenneth Williams

The French Revolution according to *Carry On.*

Follow That Camel (1967)

Dir: Gerry Thomas

Lp: Phil Silvers, Joan Sims, Kenneth Williams, Jim Dale

Beau Geste gets a makeover from the *Carry On* team.

Critics: "It all works with considerable bounce."—*Variety*

Carry On Screaming! (1966)

Dir: Gerry Thomas

Lp: Kenneth Williams, Harry H. Corbett, Fenella Fielding

Hammer Horror watch out, the Carry On gang is coming!

Finders Keepers (1966)

Dir: Sid Hayers

Lp: Cliff Richard, The Shadows, Robert Morley

The Americans lose an atomic bomb off the Spanish coast and it's found by a pop group.

Dr. Terror's House of Horrors (1965)

Dir: Freddie Francis

Lp: Peter Cushing, Ursula Howells, Alan Freeman, Roy Castle, Christopher Lee, Donald Sutherland

An eccentric who tells the fortunes of five men in a railway carriage turns out to be Death himself.

Back, left to right: **Billy Cornelius, Tom Clegg;** ***front, left to right*****: Kenneth Williams, Fenella Fielding and Harry H. Corbett in** ***Carry on Screaming!***

Carry On Cowboy (1965)

Dir: Gerry Thomas

Lp: Sid James, Joan Sims, Jim Dale, Charles Hawtrey, Kenneth Williams

The wild-wild-west according to *Carry On*.

Three Hats for Lisa (1965)

Dir: Sid Hayers

Lp: Joe Brown, Sid James, Una Stubbs
A docker and a taxi driver help a foreign film star steal three hats.

The Avengers (1965) (TV Series)
Dir: various
Lp: Patrick Macnee, Diana Rigg
The suave, sophisticated crimefighting series.

Carry On Cleo (1964)
Dir: Gerry Thomas
Lp: Sid James, Kenneth Connor, Kenneth Williams, Amanda Barrie
Cleopatra, Mark Antony and all that stuff as given the *Carry On* treatment.

Carry On Jack (1964)
Dir: Gerry Thomas
Lp: Kenneth Williams, Charles Hawtrey, Bernard Cribbins, Juliet Mills
All at sea with the gang.
Critics: "Gerald Thomas steers his cast through a maze of mix-ups and misadventures"—*Variety*

Carry On Spying (1964)
Dir: Gerry Thomas
Lp: Jim Dale, Kenneth Williams, Barbara Windsor, Bernard Cribbins
James Bond moves over for the *Carry On* gang.
Critics: "A dazzling return to form, milking every last drop from the ripe targets of espionage in general and Bond in particular"—*Sight and Sound*

The Kiss of the Vampire (1963)
Dir: Don Sharp
Lp: Noel Willman, Clifford Evans, Edward de Souza
In 1910, a Bavarian disciple of *Dracula* lures a honeymoon couple.
Critics: 'This unsubtle variation on Dracula is handled in lively fashion, with a splendid climax in which assorted white robed vampires are destroyed by bats."—Halliwell's

Carry On Cabby (1963)
Dir: Gerry Thomas
Lp: Sid James, Hattie Jacques, Charles Hawtrey, Kenneth Connor
A delightful comedy set in the world of the black cabs.

Nurse on Wheels (1963)
Dir: Gerry Thomas
Lp: Juliet Mills, Joan Sims, Ronald Lewis
Misadventures of a young district nurse.

This Is My Street (1963)
Dir: Sid Hayers

Lp: June Ritchie, Ian Hendry, John Hurt

A south London housewife embarks on an affair with her mother's lodger.

Carry On Cruising (1962)

Dir: Gerry Thomas

Lp: Kenneth Williams, Kenneth Connor, Sid James

All aboard the cruise ship for fun and hijinks with the gang.

The Iron Maiden (1962)

Dir: Gerry Thomas

Lp: Michael Craig, Alan Hale, Jr., Noel Purcell

Genevieve on a traction engine.

Twice Round the Daffodils (1962)

Dir: Gerry Thomas

Lp: Juliet Mills, Donald Sinden, Kenneth Williams

The lives of TB patients in a sanatorium.

Michael Craig shouts down instructions to get the *Iron Maiden* moving again.

Carry On Regardless (1961)

Dir: Gerry Thomas

Lp: Sid James, Kenneth Williams, Kenneth Connor, Joan Sims

The Helping Hands Agency recruits the gang for some odd jobs.

In the Doghouse (1961)

Dir: Darcy Conyers

Lp: Leslie Phillips, Hattie Jacques, James Booth, Dick Bentley

Misadventures of a newly qualified vet.

Raising the Wind (1961)

Dir: Gerry Thomas

Lp: James Robertson Justice, Leslie Phillips, Kenneth Williams, Sid James

Misadventures of students at a music academy.

No Kidding (1960)

Dir: Gerry Thomas

Lp: Leslie Phillips, Irene Handl, Joan Hickson

An old house is turned into a holiday home for deprived rich children.

Second Unit, Camera Operator, Focus and Clapper Credits

The Spy Who Loved Me (1977) (DoP: second unit)
Dir: Lewis Gilbert (John Glen, Second Unit Director)
Lp: Roger Moore, Barbara Bach, Curt Jurgens
James Bond adventure.

Shout at the Devil (1976) (DoP: second unit)
Dir: Peter Hunt (John Glen, Second Unit Director)
Lp: Roger Moore, Lee Marvin
Wilbur Smith's action-adventure in World War I Africa.

Tarzan the Magnificent (1960) (camera operator)
Dir: Robert Day
Lp: Gordon Scott, Jock Mahoney, John Carradine, Lionel Jeffries
Tarzan escorts a criminal to justice through the jungle.

Kidnapped (1960) (camera operator)
Dir: Robert Stevenson
Lp: Peter Finch, James MacArthur, Bernard Lee, Peter O'Toole.
Robert Louis Stevenson's children's adventure.

Carry On Constable (1960) (camera operator)
Dir: Gerald Thomas
Lp: Sid James, Hattie Jacques, Kenneth Williams, Charles Hawtrey, Kenneth Connor
The Carry On Gang find themselves as would-be policemen.
Critics: "An anthology of police gags and situations"—*Variety*

Watch Your Stern (1960) (camera operator)
Dir: Gerry Thomas
Lp: Kenneth Connor, Leslie Phillips, Joan Sims, Spike Milligan
A ship's steward pretends to be the inventor of a homing torpedo.

Carry On Teacher (1959) (camera operator)
Dir: Gerry Thomas
Lp: Kenneth Connor, Ted Ray, Charles Hawtrey, Hattie Jacques, Leslie Phillips
More *Carry On* mayhem set in a school.
Critics: "The laughs come readily"—*Variety*

Third Man on the Mountain (1959) (camera operator)
Dir: Ken Annakin
Lp: Michael Rennie, James MacArthur, Janet Munro, Herbert Lom
In 1865, a Swiss dishwasher has plans to conquer the local mountain.

Carry On Nurse (1958) (camera operator)
Dir: Gerry Thomas

The release poster for the fourth in the series, *Constable*.

Lp: Hattie Jacques, Kenneth Williams, Kenneth Connor, Shirley Eaton

The *Carry On* Gang in hospital.

Critics: "A seaside postcard comes to life, a shameless procession of vulgarities. Utterly irresistible."—*Sight and Sound.*

Carry On Sergeant (1958) (camera operator)
Dir: Gerry Thomas
Lp: Bob Monkhouse, Kenneth Williams, Kenneth Connor, Shirley Eaton

The first *Carry On* film, set in an Army training camp.

The Silent Enemy (1958) (camera operator)
Dir: William Fairchild
Lp: Laurence Harvey, John Clements, Michael Craig, Sid James

The World War II adventures of a naval frogman.

The Duke Wore Jeans (1958) (camera operator)
Dir: Gerry Thomas
Lp: Tommy Steele, Michael Medwin, June Laverick

An aristocrat persuades his Cockney double to woo a princess.

Time Lock (1957) (camera operator)
Dir: Gerald Thomas
Lp: Robert Beatty, Vincent Winter, Betty McDowall, Sean Connery

A small boy is trapped in a bank vault.

Vicious Circle (1957) (camera operator)
Dir: Gerald Thomas
Lp: John Mills, Derek Farr, Lionel Jeffries

An actress is found dead in Dr Latimer's flat and the murder weapon discovered in his car....

The Extra Day (1956) (camera operator)
Dir: William Fairchild
Lp: Richard Basehart, Simone Simon, Sid James

Five film extras are recalled when a scene has to be reshot.

The Green Man (1956) (camera operator)
Dir: Robert Day
Lp: Alastair Sim, George Cole, Terry-Thomas

A professional assassin stalks a pompous politician.

Three Men in a Boat (1956) (camera operator)
Dir: Ken Annakin
Lp: David Tomlinson, Jimmy Edwards, Shirley Eaton, Jill Ireland

In the 1890s, misadventures befall three men holidaying on the Thames.

Loser Takes All (1956) (camera operator)
Dir: Ken Annakin
Lp: Glynis Johns, Rossano Brazzi, Robert Morley

An accountant and his wife are invited to Monte Carlo but the high life estranges them.

Geordie (1955) (camera operator)
Dir: Frank Launder
Lp: Bill Travers, Alastair Sim, Stanley Baxter
A weakly Scottish boy takes a culture course and becomes an Olympic hammer-thrower.

The End of the Affair (1955) (camera operator)
Dir: Edward Dmytryk
Lp: Deborah Kerr, Van Johnson, Peter Cushing, John Mills
In wartime London, a woman embarks upon an affair but develops religious guilt which eventually contributes to her death.

Portrait of Alison (1955) (camera operator)
Dir: Guy Green
Lp: Robert Beatty, Terry Moore, William Sylvester
A journalist dies whilst investigating an international smuggling ring, and his brother takes up the case.

Dance Little Lady (1955) (camera operator)
Dir: Val Guest
Lp: Terence Morgan, Mai Zetterling, Eunice Gayson
An ambitious man tries to turn his balletomane daughter into a film star.

Svengali (1954) (camera operator)
Dir: Noel Langley
Lp: Hildegard Knef, Donald Wolfit, Terence Morgan
The malevolent Svengal; (Wolfit) sets his mesmerizing eye on a beautiful young woman.

Our Girl Friday (1954) (camera operator)
Dir: Noel Langley
Lp: Joan Collins, George Cole, Kenneth More, Robertson Hare
Tale about three guys marooned on a desert island with a snooty Joan Collins and a cheeky know-it-all sailor.

Rob Roy the Highland Rogue (1953) (matte effects camera operator)
Dir: Harold French
Lp: Richard Todd, Glynis Johns, Michael Gough
After the 1715 defeat of the clans, one of the highland leaders, Rob Roy MacGregor, escapes, marries and eventually becomes enough of a nuisance to George I to be outlawed and hunted by the English.

The Sword and the Rose (1953) (matte effects camera operator)
Dir: Ken Annakin
Lp: Richard Todd, Glynis Johns, James Robertson Justice
The story of Mary Tudor and her troubled path to true love. Henry VIII

determines she should wed her the King of France. She tries to flee to America with her true love. She is eventually captured. In return for her consenting to marry the King of France, Henry VIII agrees to let her choose her second husband upon his death. When King Louis of France does die, Mary is kidnapped by the Duke of Buckingham. He tries to force her to marry him but she is rescued by her love in an exciting battle on the beach.

The Story of Robin Hood and His Merry Men (1952)
(matte effects camera operator)
Dir: Ken Annakin
Lp: Richard Todd, Joan Rice, Peter Finch, James Hayter
Young Robin Hood, in love with Maid Marian, enters an archery contest with his father at the King's palace. On the way home, his father is murdered by henchmen of Prince John. Robin takes up the life of an outlaw, gathering together his band of Merry Men in Sherwood Forest

Pickwick Papers (1952) (focus puller)
Dir: Noel Langley
Lp: James Haytor, James Donald, Donald Wolfit
Dickens' novel about the adventures at the Pickwick Club brought to the screen.
Critics: "As welcome as the sun in the morning and as a British cup of tea"—*Daily Mirror*

Hotel Sahara (1951) (focus puller)
Dir: Ken Annakin
Lp: Peter Ustinov, Yvonne de Carlo, David Tomlinson
In North Africa in World War II, a small hotel changes its loyalties to suit its occupiers.

Dick Turpin's Ride (1951) (focus puller)
Dir: Ralph Murphy
Lp: Louis Hayward, Patricia Medina, John Williams
A highwayman sacrifices himself to avenge his father and protect his wife.

Prelude to Fame (1950) (focus puller)
Dir: Fergus McDonell
Lp: Jeremy Spenser, Guy Rolfe, Kathleen Ryan, Kathleen Byron
A young child with a musical talent is pushed to breaking point by an ambitious woman.

The Clouded Yellow (1950) (focus puller)
Dir: Ralph Thomas
Lp: Trevor Howard, Jean Simmons, Barry Jones
A sacked Secret Service agent gets work tending a butterfly collection and finds himself in a murder plot.

Madeleine (1949) (focus puller)
Dir: David Lean
Lp: Ann Todd, Leslie Banks, Elizabeth Sellers

A young woman in Victorian Glasgow is accused of murder, but the verdict is "not proven."

Passionate Friends (1948) (focus puller)
Dir: David Lean
Lp: Ann Todd, Trevor Howard, Claude Rains

A woman marries an older man only to meet again her young lover.
Critics: "Mr. Lean plants his clues with the certainty of a master of a detective story, and heightens their effect with a sure handling of camera and sound-track"—The Times

Oliver Twist (1948) (focus puller)
Dir: David Lean
Lp: Alec Guinness, Robert Newton, John Howard Davies, Kay Walsh

The classic Dickens novel of how a young orphan falls in among thieves but is later saved.

Critics: "A brilliant, fascinating movie, no less a classic than the Dickens novel which it brings to life"—*Time*

1944–1945 Photographer in Fleet Air Services

Tawney Pipit (1944) (clapper boy)
Dir: Bernard Miles
Lp: Bernard Miles, Rosamund John, Jean Gillie

A young Alan Hume, getting to grips with the camera at the beginning of his long career.

The life of a village in wartime is disrupted when two rare birds nest in a local meadow.

Critics: "Not quite dry enough for the epicures nor sweet enough for the addicts."—C.A. Lejeune

The Flemish Farm (1943) (clapper boy)
Dir: Jeffrey Dell
Lp: Clive Brook, Clifford Evans, Jane Baxter

An attempt is made to retrieve a buried flag from occupied Belgium.

Critics: "Tolerable wartime flagwaver"—*Halliwell's*

In Which We Serve (1942) (clapper boy)
Dir: Noël Coward, David Lean
Lp: Noël Coward, Bernard Miles, John Mills, Richard Attenborough

Survivors from a torpedoed destroyer recall their life at sea.

Critics: "One of the screen's proudest achievements at any time and in any country."—*Newsweek*

Thunder Rock (1942) (clapper boy)
Dir: Roy Boulting
Lp: Michael Redgrave, Lilli Palmer, Barbara Mullen, James Mason, Finlay Currie

A journalist disgusted with the world of the 1930s retires to a lighthouse on Lake Michigan and is haunted by the ghosts of immigrants drowned there a century before.

Critics: "Boldly imaginative in theme and treatment"—*Sunday Express* "More interesting technically than anything since *Citizen Kane*"—*Manchester Guardian*

The First of the Few (1942) (clapper boy)
Dir: Leslie Howard
Lp: Leslie Howard, David Niven, Rosamund John, Roland Culver, David Horne

The story of R.J. Mitchell, who devised the Spitfire just ahead of the onset of World War II.

Critics: "Full of action, Schneider Trophy races, test flying and flashes from the Battle of Britain."—*The Sunday Times*

Index

Numbers in *italics* refer to pages with photographs.